THE MODERN LIBRARY

of the World's Best Books

»»»»»»»»»»»»»»»»»»»»»»»»»»»»»»»»

A NEW ANTHOLOGY OF MODERN POETRY

A NEW ANTHOLOGY OF
MODERN POETRY

>>

EDITED, WITH AN INTRODUCTION
BY SELDEN RODMAN

>>

THE MODERN LIBRARY
NEW YORK

THE MODERN LIBRARY

IS PUBLISHED BY

RANDOM HOUSE, INC.

BENNETT A. CERF · DONALD S. KLOPFER · ROBERT K. HAAS

Manufactured in the United States of America

Printed by Parkway Printing Company Paper by Richard Bauer & Co.

Bound by H. Wolff

Acknowledgments

For permission to use the copyrighted poems included in this volume, acknowledgment is made to the following publishers and poets:

Brandt & Brandt
for "Moriturus," by Edna St. Vincent Millay from *The Buck in the Snow,* published by Harper & Brothers. Copyright, 1928, by Edna St. Vincent Millay
for "Litany for Dictatorships," by Stephen Vincent Benét from *Burning City,* published by Farrar & Rinehart, Inc. Copyright, 1933, 1935, 1936, by Stephen Vincent Benét
for "Thomas Jefferson," "John Quincy Adams," "Daniel Boone" and "Abraham Lincoln" from *A Book of Americans,* published by Farrar & Rinehart, Inc. Copyright, 1933, by Stephen Vincent and Rosemary Benét

Albert & Charles Boni, Inc.
for two selections from *Blues: An Anthology*

Eunice Clark
for "The People Has No Obituary"

Sarah N. Cleghorn
for selections from *Threescore*

Common Sense
for "The Road from Election to Christmas" by Oscar Williams
for "Millions Are Learning How" by James Agee
for "Standard Forgings Plant" by William Stephens

Covici-Friede, Inc.
for "Homage to Literature" and "Boy with His Hair Cut Short" from *U.S.1* by Muriel Rukeyser

Malcolm Cowley
for "The Hill above the Mine" and "For St. Bartholomew's Eve"

Coward-McCann, Inc.
for "These Are the Live" from *Angel Arms* by Kenneth Fearing

Curtis Brown, Ltd.
for "Lines in Dispraise of Dispraise," "Song of the Open Road," "Autres Bêtes, Autres Moeurs" by Ogden Nash

The Dial Press, Inc.
for "The Serf" by Roy Campbell

Dodd, Mead & Company
for "The Ballad of Jesse James" by William Rose Benét
for lines from "The Great Lover" and "Wagner" by Rupert Brooke

Doubleday, Doran & Company
for the selection from *American Song* by Paul Engle

E. P. Dutton & Company
for "On the Vanity of Earthly Greatness" by Arthur Guiterman

Esquire
for "Consuelo at the Country Club" by Selden Rodman

Farrar & Rinehart, Inc.
for "Canto XVII" by Ezra Pound
for "Pole Star for This Year" by Archibald MacLeish
for "Consuelo at the Country Club" by Selden Rodman
for "Litany for Dictatorships" by Stephen Vincent Benét and Four Rhymes from *A Book of Americans* by Stephen Vincent and Rosemary Benét

Kenneth Fearing
for "Dirge" from *Poems*

Archibald Fleming
for "Speech of the First Sentry"

The Forum
for "Report" by Archibald Fleming
for "Rapid Transit" by James Agee

Harcourt, Brace & Company
for selections from *The People, Yes* by Carl Sandburg
for selections from *Collected Poems* by E. E. Cummings
for "I Paint What I See" by E. B. White from *The New Yorker Book of Verse*
for selections from *The Rock* and *Collected Poems* by T. S. Eliot
for "Tombstone with Cherubim" and "Salvos for Randolph Bourne" from *No Retreat* by Horace Gregory

Harper & Brothers
for "The Conspirators" by Frederic Prokosch
for "Moriturus" from *The Buck in the Snow* by Edna St. Vincent Millay

Henry Holt & Company
for "The Listeners" by Walter de la Mare
for "The Fear" and "Two Tramps in Mud Time" by Robert Frost
for "Others, I am not the first," "1887," and "Terence, This is Stupid Stuff" from *The Shropshire Lad* by A. E. Housman

Houghton Mifflin Company
for selections from *Collected Poems* and *Conquistador* by Archibald MacLeish
for "Little Ivory Figures Pulled with String" by Amy Lowell

Alfred A. Knopf, Inc.
for selections from *Harmonium* by Wallace Stevens
for "Here Lies a Lady" from *Chills and Fever* by John Crowe Ransom
for "The Elephant Is Slow to Mate" from *Pansies* by D. H. Lawrence
for "Wild Peaches" and "Castilian" from *The Collected Poems of Elinor Wylie*

Liveright Publishing Corporation
for selections from *Collected Poems* by Hart Crane

Hugh MacDiarmid
for "Reflections in an Ironworks" and "At the Cenotaph"

The Macmillan Company
for selections from *Selected Poems* by Marianne Moore
for lines from "Reynard the Fox" by John Masefield
for "Afterwards" by Thomas Hardy
for selections from *Collected Poems* by William Butler Yeats
for selections from *Collected Poems* by Vachel Lindsay
for "The Man Against the Sky" by Edwin Arlington Robinson

Edwin Markham
for "The Man with the Hoe"

Edgar Lee Masters
for "Mrs. Williams," "Chandler Nicholas," "Howard Lamson" from *Spoon River Anthology* and *New Spoon River*

The Nation
for "Fallow Land" by Eunice Clark

New Masses
for "Death of a Craneman" by Alfred Hayes
for "The Eyes Have It" by William Stephens

The New Republic
From *Dusk of the Gods* by S. Funaroff
for "The Yachts" by William Carlos Williams from *An Early Martyr*

Oxford University Press
for "Johannas Milton, Senex" by Robert Bridges
for "Pied Beauty," "Duns Scotus's Oxford," "Fragment" and "Felix Randal" by Gerard Manley Hopkins

Random House, Inc.
for "Roan Stallion," "Shine, Perishing Republic" and "Practical People" by Robinson Jeffers
for "The Express," "I think continually of those who were truly great," "From all these events, from the slump, from the war, from the boom," "The Funeral" and "oh young men oh young comrades" by Stephen Spender

for "Tempt me no more" and "Consider these, for we have condemned them" by C. Day Lewis

for "Get there if you can and see the land," "Sir, no man's enemy, forgiving all," "The Airman's Alphabet," Chorus from *The Dog Beneath the Skin,* Chorus from *The Ascent of F 6* and "Prologue" by W. H. Auden

for "Museums" and "Their Last Will and Testament" by Louis MacNeice

Edwin Rolfe

for "Definition" from *To My Contemporaries*

Delmore Schwartz

for "For One Who Would Not Take His Life in His Hands"

Charles Scribner's Sons

for "Miniver Cheevy" and "George Crabbe" by Edwin Arlington Robinson

for "Prelude LVI" by Conrad Aiken

for "Idiot" from *Selected Poems* by Allen Tate

Sedgwick and Jackson, Ltd.

for "In Time Like Glass" by Walter James Turner

Simon and Schuster, Inc.

for "Final Autumn" from *Year's End* by Josephine W. Johnson

Spirit

for "The Elements" by Oscar Williams

Stackpole Sons

For a selection from *The River* by Pare Lorentz

Viking Press

for "I hear an army charging upon the land" by James Joyce

for "The Sea" and a selection from "The Ship of Death" by D. H. Lawrence

for selections from *The Book of American Negro Spirituals*

for "John Henry tol' his Cap'n" from *Rolling Along in Song* by J. Rosamond Johnson

for "The Legion of Iron" by Lola Ridge

for "Song of Songs," "The Show," "Arms and the Boy," "Strange Meeting," "Greater Love," "Disabled," and "To My Friend" by Wilfred Owen
for "Last Speech to the Court" by Bartolomeo Vanzetti from *The Letters of Sacco and Vanzetti*
for "Fighting Words" and "Bohemia" by Dorothy Parker
for selections from *Lawrence: The Last Crusade* by Selden Rodman

Ann Watkins, Inc.
for "The Return" and "The River-Merchant's Wife" by Ezra Pound

Yale University Press
for "The Trial," "City of Monuments" and "Citation for Horace Gregory" by Muriel Rukeyser

J. P. Wade
for "A Hymn to No One Body"

Contents

PART TWO

Introduction

BY SELDEN RODMAN

Modern poetry, like all other poetry, is a language devised to communicate those experiences or ideas which defy the deliberate order and pace of prose. The most intense prose, whatever advantage in explicit presentation it may have over all but the greatest verse, is less highly charged with suggestive ambiguity and direct tonal quality than the special language we attempt to describe by the word poetry.

What is modern poetry, and where does it begin? Did it begin in America with Edgar Allan Poe? It certainly began in France toward the middle of the nineteenth century when the younger poets rejected the romanticism of Victor Hugo as inadequate protest against what they considered the anti-poetic materialism of "bourgeois" civilization. But these first poets of the ivory tower—Baudelaire, Rimbaud, Verlaine, Laforgue, Mallarmé—didn't start to influence English poetry until the time of Yeats, and not with any widespread effect until after the War. Symbolism, then—the highly personal, associative approach which these poets invented, and which demands further discussion later on—is an important (perhaps the most important) element in modern poetry, but it is only one. It doesn't cover the totally different revolt against tradition in America that began with Whitman and survives in Sandburg. Nor do such modern poets as Hopkins and Housman, Elinor Wylie and Edna St. Vincent Millay, Masefield and Hardy and Frost have anything to do with it.

Unless the tradition of starting a modern anthology with Walt Whitman or Emily Dickinson is promptly violated, the term "modern" will lose what little meaning it still has. Whitman and Dickinson are modern to be sure—but so are Blake and Marvell and Donne. The demarcation of modernity is a personal matter at best. So let me be arbitrary and start somewhere else.

W. B. Yeats (who is still alive in both senses) not only knew Gerard Manley Hopkins before his death in 1888, he also attended the famous Tuesday receptions at the apartment of Stephen Mallarmé in Paris *fin de siècle*. There also came the young Valéry. And there symbolist innovation became symbolist doctrine. Ten years later John Masefield, establishing another link with the past, tells us that he was stimulated by the Monday evenings at the London home of W. B. Yeats. Later he would go to the reading room of the British Museum, where he would see that incorrigible old Victorian, Swinburne, deaf and roaring to himself over some obscene impropriety.

Chronologically I have begun with Hopkins, whose

poems (though written outside of any tradition whatsoever in the seventies and eighties) appeared in my generation and have had their first influence, already a considerable one, on the very youngest living poets. Otherwise my superficial criterion has been simply whether the poet lived and wrote in the twentieth century—with Carroll's "Jabberwocky" as the single irrepressible exception.

I say "superficial" because obviously a more important test has been whether the poet, or the poem, seemed "modern" to me. What has my test been? A simple definition, broad enough to be comprehensive, would be too broad to be sensible. I shall therefore list a few of what seem to me the characteristics of "modernity," though it may be difficult to dissociate some of them from the hallmarks of true poetry at any time. However—

imagery patterned increasingly on everyday speech

absence of inversions, stilted apostrophes, conventional end-rhymes, "poetic" language generally, except where used deliberately for incantatory effect

freedom from the ordinary logic of sequence, jumping from one image to the next by association *rather than by the usual cause-effect method*

emphasis on the ordinary, in reaction against the traditional poetic emphasis on the cosmic

concern with naked consciousness and the newly identified "unconscious" as against "the soul" concern with the common man, almost to the exclusion of the "hero" or extraordinary man

concern with the social order as against "heaven" and "nature"

A few of the poets, like Housman, answer only to the most general of these criteria. But these few have contributed nothing to technical innovation or fresh outlook, and for that reason have had no significant influence.

II. THE ARRANGEMENT

To avoid rigidity, I have given no titles to the four sections into which this anthology is divided. Their contents should speak for them. The introductory poems sound off. But lest any esoteric pretension be inferred—roughly:

In the first part are the forerunners of contemporary poetry as well as certain poets and poems that belong to no classifiable tradition.

Clearly the second embraces the poets who derive their inspiration from the people and the soil, in rebellion for the rights of both, but rebelling in a broader, possibly more traditional way than the poets included in IV.

While Yeats himself was influenced not a little by the French symbolist movement, it was not until Pound and Eliot that the whole course of modern verse was transformed by it. Here then is Part III. Pound has been something of a scholar in the Latin, Provençal, Italian and Chinese, as well as in the symbolist language. He has lived in self-imposed exile for twenty years. It is fitting that he should come first here. Eliot, whose use of symbolism has been more deliberate and intellectual, has had the largest influence of any living poet, though already that influence has gone beyond the point where it is a healthy one. I have concluded the section with Gregory and MacLeish whose styles are clearly evolved from this movement, but whose growing social consciousness marks a distinct finish to the exile and ivory-tower phases of symbolism.

Part IV, in a sense, brings together the matter of II and the manner of III, but in addition many new things of its own. Here, for the first time, the influence of Hopkins' "sprung rhythm" [1] will be felt. Satire assumes new strength and importance, especially in the work of W. H. Auden. Revolt against society will drive revolt against form into the background. And the new synthesis (social-symbolism, we might call it) will inevitably seem less sharply original, if more outspoken and robust.

The number of poems by which a poet is represented should not necessarily be taken as a judgment of his relative importance. I feel that Frost and Pound, for

[1] This form, occasionally used in old ballads, by Langland in *Piers Ploughman,* and by Milton in the choruses of *Samson Agonistes,* has the advantage of opening up verse to include easily scientific words and conversational rhythms; its principal defect is the indeterminacy of the stress, since the stresses rather than the syllables are counted. One foot may have one or many syllables.

example, are fairly represented by two or three poems, while Yeats, whose style has undergone a great many changes, is inadequately represented by five. "Two Tramps in Mud Time" is indeed such a perfect example of Frost's philosophy and art that it might almost represent him entirely by itself. Other poems have not been chosen as representative of the poet at all. They may have seemed excellent in themselves; or they may have so well exemplified the persistence of a certain tradition that they seemed to fill an organic place in the book. May I assure the reader—and the poet—that there is nothing invidious intended by the inclusion of a poem in this Part or that? Poems that appeal particularly to the editor himself—"Castilian," "Two Tramps in Mud Time," "Burying Ground by the Ties," "I think continually of those who were truly great"—are to be found in all sections. Nor is any judgment of superiority hinted by the merely historical fact that most of the younger poets today express their social convictions under the influence of symbolism and hence fall within the final grouping.

The scheme is largely chronological, but by no means entirely. Thus Wilfred Owen, in my opinion the noblest voice in English poetry since the death of Keats, speaks only through force of circumstances of the particular injustice of war. He was killed in 1918 and the necessarily split allegiance of true poets since his time was forecast in the memorable words of his "Introduction": "Above all I am not concerned with Poetry. My subject is War and the pity of War. The Poetry is in the pity . . . All a poet can do today is warn."

III. TAKING POETRY OFF THE SHELF

The two outstanding anthologists of recent years have been Louis Untermeyer and Conrad Aiken. Untermeyer has been notable for his catholic taste (the most recent edition of *Modern American and British Poetry* contains no fewer than 1,604 poems). Aiken has been distinguished by his discriminating partiality to the "metaphysical" poets. Very broadly their works reflect two viewpoints: that of the New Poetry (heralded by the Chicago "renaissance" of 1912), and that of the Lost Generation whose roots extended back even beyond symbolism to the so-called metaphysical poets like Donne.

Neither of these anthologists has shown much favor to the significant new poetry of social protest. Neither has included any folk-verse. Both have favored the lyric almost to the exclusion of the characteristic narrative and epic poetry of our time. Both anthologists have suffered, in my opinion, from an excess of high seriousness; there is hardly a humorous poem or even representation of light verse in the collections of either. Yet:

> *"According to his powers each may give;*
> *Only on varied diet can we live . . .*
> *The pious fable and the dirty story*
> *Share in the total literary glory."*

And one of the major blocks to the popular appreciation of poetry, especially modern poetry, is the conviction that it must be Highly Serious—and consequently Highly Dull. People who dislike the very idea of poetry, says Auden, dislike it as they dislike over-earnest people, "they imagine it is always worrying about the eternal verities. . . . Poetry is no better and no worse than human nature; it is profound and shallow, sophisticated and naïve, dull and witty, bawdy and chaste in turn."

So, I think, the haunting songs of the Negro people, the Benéts' verse for children, the bitter *vers de société* of Dorothy Parker, the raucous rhymes of Ogden Nash, the parodies and ballads, when phrased with a master's precision, help to make up what is poetry in our time.

IV. THE EXCITEMENT OF POETRY

To read poetry, however, and get the best out of it, does require effort. Poetry may be read on several levels —for its sound, for its content, for its pith, for excitement or for relaxation. But those who read it for merely sentimental reasons, the associations and the pleasing cadences, can hardly expect a visitation of the famous trouble Housman used to have with his beard and razor when a line of poetry strayed into his mind. "The sentimentalists," says Yeats, "are practical people who believe in money, in position, in a marriage bell, and whose understanding of happiness is to be so busy, whether at work or at play, that all is forgotten but the momentary aim." The aim of poetry is not momentary, though its enjoyment may be. Its full enjoyment is lasting, precisely because it is not written by sentimentalists.

I will mention a few of the many things that are exciting to me in the poems of this collection, not because my reactions are important to anyone but myself, but because they may help some readers to look for other specific things themselves.

I would call attention at random to the *speed* of Masefield's lines, to the dropping sensation induced by the step-like arrangement of vowel sounds in the line

"Then down on the mile-long green decline."

I would call attention to exciting transitions like that of the first line of the fourth sonnet in Elinor Wylie's "Wild Peaches," where the lush, dreamy South suddenly becomes the austere, bitten North. Or the sixteenth and seventeenth lines of Yeats' "Dedication" stanzas, where anger suddenly flares up and as suddenly subsides.

I would mention the broken last line of the seventh Negro spiritual, where the effect of a sob and of defiance poignantly mingle. Or the tempo, shifting like magic from disgust to ecstasy in Cummings' "i go to this window." Or the electric effect of the rhyme on the last word of Fleming's "Speech of the Sentry."

Assonance [2] is not new in Wilfred Owen, but it is employed by him to extraordinary effect:

[2] The use of imperfect rhyme, where the consonants but not the vowels of the end-words are similar.

"They will be swift with swiftness of the tigress,
None will break ranks, though nations trek from progress.
Courage was mine, and I had mystery,
Wisdom was mine and I had mastery . . ."

Observe the "lift" in the sprung rhythm of Spender's limpid verse, the combination of delicacy, nobility and tensile strength:

"It is too late to stay in great houses where the ghosts are prisoned . . .
Oh comrades, step beautifully from the solid wall
advance to rebuild and sleep with friend on hill"

Or the effect of clean distinction when life is breathed into old words under the impact of new ideas—by Muriel Rukeyser's

"Before they die the brave have set their hand
On rich particular beauty for their heirs . . ."

Do these examples seem trivial? Is it a poor definition that a poet's stature may be measured by the number of quotable lines he has written? Of such small things is the stuff of poetry fashioned. . . . But the "grand manner" is no more absent from modern poetry than from any other poetry. You will find it in the conclusion to "Felix Randal" when Hopkins suddenly passes from the pathetic details of his friend's illness to the triumph of his homely deeds. Or in the magnificent peroration of Auden's vision of a future England:

"As when Merlin, tamer of horses, and his lords to whom
Stonehenge was still a thought, the Pillars passed
And into the undared ocean swung north their prow,
Drives through the night and star-concealing dawn
For the virgin roadsteads of our hearts an unwavering keel."

V. IS MODERN POETRY DIFFICULT?

If it is the business of poetry not merely to convey information, but to provide for the reader precisely those "vibrations" experienced by the writer, is it small wonder that the demand upon the reader's sensitivity and concentration is equally great? Shall we be shocked to find that much poetry in every age has been "difficult"? And is it surprising that for the *full* absorption of any poetry as much attention and understanding are required as an intelligent music-lover will devote to the intricate structure of a piece of music? Yet superficially the music, like the poem, may be enjoyable to everyone who hears it. For like music "poetry often communicates when one does not understand it, and even when written in a language which one knows very imperfectly."

There has been difficult poetry in every age, then. But in periods of transition and social upheaval, when ideas, attitudes and even language are uprooted or in process of reconstruction, poetry has been correspondingly complex. That it has proved, at such times, to be correspondingly rewarding, is a fact that has sometimes been left to later generations to discover. Such epochs, and our own is no exception, have produced plenty of poetry that may be enjoyed with a minimum of effort. And the most subtle practitioners in such a period, as witness James Joyce in our own, have occasionally written with piercing directness. But the fact of complexity remains.

What Shakespeare, writing at the peak of the English Renaissance, meant by the words

> *"When steel grows soft as is the parasite's silk*
> *Let him be made an overture for the wars!"*

I am sure I do not know. Nor does Shelley's

> *"Pinnacled dim in the intense inane"*

convey any particular image today. Shelley, the poet of the French Revolution, was doubtless making a supreme attempt to fix something which troubled the romantic conscience, but it proved no more successful than the lines

> *"Sir, no man's enemy, forgiving all*
> *But will his negative inversion, be prodigal"*

which open a poem I have thought otherwise fine enough to include in this collection. "If a poet writes entirely in metaphor, using rare words only," said Aristotle at a time when poetry was going through another of its periodic crises, "the result is jargon." "But," he wisely added, "he who uses merely commonplace words sacrifices all to clarity."

VI. IS SYMBOLISM TO BLAME?

People who try to do new things, or even old things in a new way, are never popular. There is nothing revolutionary in the sentiment of the following as we read it now:

"Come, Muse, migrate from Greece and Ionia,
Cross out please those immensely overpaid accounts,
That matter of Troy and Achilles' wrath . . .
Placard 'Remove' and 'To Let' on the rocks of your
snowy Parnassus"

—but imagine the feelings that must have been hurt by the language no less than the sentiment in Whitman's classic-fronted day!

Even so in our time the audience for poetry, necessarily limited at any time, has been jolted by some poets and inexcusably badgered by others, until one author complained that the act of publication was like dropping a rose petal in the Grand Canyon and waiting to hear the echo.

Let us admit at once that two characteristics of postwar verse have stood between the poets and a healthy audience: a philosophy of isolation and a private language.

The first of these began in France in the mid-nineteenth century when artists, as we observed, were expressing their revolt by retiring into some form of ideal dream-world of their own making. Great poets, intense but too isolated to contribute to the development of a tradition in accord with the new social and scientific facts, rose on the crest of this first symbolist tide. One of them, Rimbaud, carried his escape so far as to anticipate such a recent phenomenon as surrealism. The following passage from his most mature work is self-explanatory—and prophetic:

> "One must be modern completely . . . I loved meaningless door-tops, backgrounds, acrobats' back-cloths, signboards, popular prints, old-fashioned literature, church Latin, misspelled erotica, . . . I invented the color of the vowels! —A black, E white, I red, O blue, U green . . . I accustomed myself to simple hallucination: I saw quite freely a mosque in place of a factory, a school of drums made by the angels, a drawing room at the bottom of a lake . . . I finished by finding the disorder of my senses sacred."

Poets who followed him, if they did not carry their burden to the same extremity, were content to develop some particular facet of the hard symbolist jewel.

Paul Valéry, for example, has battened upon the precious myth of the poet's unproductivity. Self-consciously he will work upon a single poem for years and years, treating it as a piece of sculpture to be admired for its form only. Ruling out verse that is full of passion or deliberately intelligible, he likens poetry to a heavy load which the poet carts to the roof bit by bit and then drops all at once on the poor unsuspecting reader who passes by below. "Enthusiasm," he states, "is not an artist's state of mind." And small wonder that the puritanism of this doctrine (which finds its American spokesman in the person of Mr. Allen Tate) is capable of awakening small enthusiasm in the reading public!

But symbolism, as I have endeavored to show in explaining the arrangement of the present collection, is not a piece of eccentric baggage to be tossed overboard lightly. For better or worse, it is part of the structure of the ship. And modern poetry, unless we would scuttle it entirely, must be an intricate, nicely balanced vessel if it is to ride the troubled cross-currents of our world.

VII. WHAT MAKES IT OBSCURE?

If the philosophy of much modern poetry contributed to isolating it from all but a priesthood, the language which that philosophy called into being acted as a still more serious deterrent. For the style was bound to persist long after the attitudes themselves became unfashionable. Thus, for example, much of what has loosely been called "proletarian" poetry is written (ironically) in the same private, filigree manner with which the poet was wont to embellish the interior of his ivory tower.

C. Day Lewis [3] has pointed to the association-of-ideas technique, employed by T. S. Eliot and his followers, as a major cause of obscurity in post-war poetry. The poet takes over a sequence of images from psychology's exploration of the "unconscious"—and then presents them *as in psychic life* without the logical connections.

Another source of obscurity is the modern poet's attempt to compete with the clanging rhythms and inchoate life of the city. This often leads, when the material is badly digested, to more confusion than one finds even in the poet who deliberately escapes from the city into a private, pastoral world of his own. Furthermore the city poet, often finding himself isolated from any genuine contact with his fellows, fails to derive that benefit from the group which has fructified art in all periods of great achievement. At such a time, he finds himself necessarily talking to the small group that can readily share his experiences.

VIII. DOES SCIENCE CONFLICT WITH IT?

Every five years or so, somebody announces in a solemn voice that poetry is dead. Coleridge, great romantic that he was, started the critics off a hundred years ago

[3] A short list of the best studies of modern poetry, for which this introduction may serve, at best, as a summary, might include Mr. Lewis' *A Hope for Poetry, Axel's Castle* by Edmund Wilson, *Hart Crane* by Philip Horton, *The Name and Nature of Poetry* by A. E. Housman, *This Modern Poetry* by Babette Deutsch and Stephen Spender's *The Destructive Element.*

when he announced that poetry, in opposition to science, was after pleasure, rather than truth. Even so astute a critic as Edmund Wilson has fallen victim to this delusion. Ten years ago he shook his head when T. S. Eliot ventured the belief that poetry would be reinstated on the stage. Today, with that minor miracle on the way to accomplishment (by Eliot himself, among others), Mr. Wilson sadly notes the decline of Edna St. Vincent Millay and informs us that prose, and prose alone, is the medium of the future.

Both of these arguments arise from a fundamental misconception of the role of poetry. Poetry, as Hart Crane said, is an architectural art "based not on Evolution or the idea of progress, but on the articulation of the contemporary human consciousness *sub specie aeternitatis,* and inclusive of all readjustments incident to science and other shifting factors related to that consciousness." The function of poetry in this age is similar to its function in any age; and it is notable that the machine is being assimilated by the younger poets today with far less self-consciousness than by Crane himself—and for the very reasons which he himself described with such insight:

> "The emotional stimulus of machinery is on an entirely different psychic plane from that of poetry. Its only menace lies in its capacities for facile entertainment, so easily accessible as to arrest the development of any but the most negligible aesthetic responses . . . Unless poetry can absorb the machine, i.e., *acclimatize* it as naturally and casually as trees, cattle, galleons, castles and all the other

human associations of the past, then poetry has failed of its full contemporary function. This process does not infer any program nor does it essentially involve even the specific mention of a single mechanical contrivance. It demands, however, along with the traditional qualifications of the poet, an extraordinary capacity for surrender, at least temporarily, to the sensations of urban life. . . ."

Max Eastman, one of the leading literary worshippers of science, maintains that science has withdrawn intellect from literature. He goes so far as to say that nothing is left for the poets but to sing. "It is not their function to conceive things truly but to live them vividly." But while ignoring completely the role of poetry in "articulating contemporary human consciousness" and giving form to it, Mr. Eastman disregards an almost equally important function of the poet. Science does not and cannot make men feel, much less act. Nor does science as such, any more than sociology as such, give modern man that confidence in his own dignity and essential nobility which is necessary for the translation of mere animal energy into aspirations, aspirations into deeds. A great scientist must be a poet also. He must have vision to go beyond precepts and conceive what never was. But a great poet need not be a scientist, though his mind must have equal integrity, daring and orderliness. "No amount of psychological experimentation," a leading modern biologist has said, "can reveal the profundities of an emotional situation like a single poem."

A great scientist or a great prophet or a great revolutionary must have a one-track mind. For the success of his enterprise, his dedication must be complete. When Millikan writes of religion or politics he writes as a child. Lenin, according to Maxim Gorky, listened to a Beethoven Sonata with a feeling of guilt—"It affects your nerves, makes you want to say stupid, nice things and stroke the heads of people who could create such beauty while living in this vile hell."

But a poet must be a whole man, else he will never see the relationship between things, the dualities and incongruities, yes, and the permanencies that make poetry. Imagine this scene. An old man, poorly clad, totters down the steps of a library with his eyes fixed ahead of him. Our three "doers"—the scientist, statesman and priest—will want to do something about him, and quite rightly. They will prescribe medicine, old-age pensions or prayer, as the case may be. But the poet, while acknowledging the necessity for some of these remedies, is not looking primarily for a "cure." His poem may end with an exhortation, bidding the old man shake his fist as he did in his youth, but he will see the situation symbolically. He may see the futility of years of knowledge which have left the old man still staring blankly into the void. He may see the unconquerable impulse that sends him to the library with his remaining strength. Or he may see him as one in whose veins, quickened by the passionate lines of some other poet, blossom again dimly remembered Springs.

In any case one may be sure that the poet who captures the incident in any one of its symbolic relationships will, if he does so intensely, communicate something to the reader that the reader will never get from a description indicated in terms of its "cure." The cure, if there is one, comes afterward. If the reader's sensibilities have been moved, his will may be charged also. At the very least, the lens of his eye will have been adjusted to receive more daylight. For art, along with science, is one of the valid ways of communicating knowledge about reality. And it is even quite possible, as one scientist has suggested, that tomorrow, following this era in which materialistic conceptions have proven inadequate in the very fields where they achieved their greatest triumphs, "values will be regarded as inherent in reality."

IX. DOES PROPAGANDA CANCEL IT?

Shall we infer from this that "propaganda" has no place in poetry? That aesthetic values are to be independent of all other values? Shall we agree with the early T. S. Eliot, for instance, that moral, didactic, emotional, religious, historical and political purposes are the spheres of prose alone—purposes *in spite of which* "poetry" has sometimes emerged and survived? Shall we concur in his pedantic definition of poetry as "not a turning loose of emotion, but an escape from emotion; not an expression of personality, but an escape from personality?" Of course the definition may be applied to

Mr. Eliot, who, it is generally admitted, "was born middle-aged and has not been getting any younger since" —but try to imagine Stephen Spender without emotion, Robert Frost without personality!

I think we are getting away from this most unhistorical view of poetry today. We acknowledge, to be sure, that religious fervor and "correct" politics do not necessarily produce poetry. But we observe that the very greatest poetry, and certainly the most monumental, was written by men who paraded their extra-aesthetic intentions and who, if they were not actually out to instruct, were certainly anxious to expound.

It is even possible that we are returning to Matthew Arnold's rather heavy view of poetry as "criticism of life in which our race, as time goes on, will find an ever surer and surer stay"—but I think not. This definition is as narrow on the moral side as Eliot's is on the aesthetic. For though it is true, as Spender says, that the greatest art is moral "even when the artist has no particular axe to grind," and that in revolutionary times issues of war and peace and social justice tend to make issues of private morality, theft and manners almost insignificant—poetry, to remain poetry, must deal with all of these larger questions in terms of the emotions generated by them, in terms of human values rather than "party lines"; it must stand on the plane of *choice* where tragedy or acceptance are the alternatives, rather than on the plane of *conversion* where the poles are heresy and conformity only.

Propaganda is concerned with telling people what to do; poetry, at least the social poetry that is generated in times like ours, with "extending our knowledge of good and evil, perhaps making the necessity for action more urgent, and its nature more clear." Where the mind is still free, neither complacent nor shackled to the past nor servile to the discipline of the future, there will poetry flourish.

X. THE FUTURE

The most demanding, but the most rewarding view of the poet's function that we have is Emerson's. The poet, he said, is the "complete man" who "apprises us not of his wealth, but of the commonwealth." In recent years we have strayed far from this definition—to poetry's loss and the poet's, as well as the public's. If we have come to regard poetry as something to be taken with breathless ceremony on the rarest of occasions, it is because we have ceased to think of the poet as "the utterer of the necessary and the casual."

In a sensuous world ever-present and ever-beautiful, it is the poet who should affirm the fact so sharply that we are called upon to live vividly ourselves. He will affirm the good in the very teeth of man's inhumanity to man, without minimizing the corrupt. A painter may get along with his eyes, a sculptor with his touch, a musician with his ear; but a poet must add to each one of these perceptions *intellect*. "The experience of each new age requires a new confession," and the utterance of that confession in such an unequivocal medium as language requires every instrument in expression's orchestra. "It is not metres," said Emerson, "but a metre-making argument that makes a poem." And seldom in history has a people been faced with more urgent arguments.

If anybody should be above the battle, it is the poet. If anybody should be *in* the battle, it is he. He alone must take sides and still reserve half his sympathy for the enemy. His heart must be involved, but his mind clear as spring water.

Nothing can be too ugly, too sordid, too brutal, too immediate, too mean to evoke the poet's interest. Yet his own sensibilities must be incorruptible; he must be virtuous, if not chaste; devout without subscribing to creeds; humble, but not pious. "On the brink of the waters of life and truth" we may be miserably dying, but the poet, if he comes down, as Milton urged, from the wine and generous living of his natural state to drink water out of a wooden bowl, may impart life to a whole generation . . .

We Americans should be proud of our poetry, but we are not. Poe and Emerson, Whitman, Emily Dickinson and Frost, Vachel Lindsay and Eliot, the anonymous authors of the spirituals and chanteys, have contributed to the literature of the world. What other art in America can say as much? Yet we honor poetry, if at all, with a jingling column in the morning paper, stuff it in the cracks of a magazine as a space-filler, at best pay perfunctory homage once a year with a professors' prize.

The poet himself is looked at askance; we are not quite sure it is a man's job he is doing. It is safe enough to admire the professional rabbit-poetry of the prize winners. But a Hemingway or a Sandburg, who has been photographed with a fishing-tackle or guitar, is accepted almost in spite of his literary accomplishments. It would be an almost insurmountable handicap if a man in public life were discovered, like a Milton or a Lorenzo de' Medici, to write good poetry.

Our poets themselves take refuge from notoriety in a double life, or, like Jeffers, seal themselves away from the reeking herd in some rock-bound fastness. The communication and integration of ideas that New England knew in Emerson's time is a long way from us. Yet this community of experience has been a phenomenon of every creative epoch from Athens and Rome to Florence, Weimar, Paris and London.

Only very recently, in the brotherhood of the younger English poets, is there a portent of change. Its immediate effect has been not only to stimulate the leaders of this group themselves, but to attract to their community a number of lesser talents, quickening their production, quantitatively and qualitatively, increasing their self-confidence. If we can come out of our puritan closets in America once more without hopping the first boat for Montparnasse, I think we have far greater potentialities for a rich, vital national literature in America. Our manner of speech is necessarily more "public." Our traditions are less smothering, the very resources of our land are more promising; we do not yet live in stifling apprehension between one war and the next. The country that was big enough for Poe and Whitman at the same time, is still big enough.

Our younger poets have taken the first step. They are beginning, as I believe the last part of this anthology will indicate, to fuse the naturalistic and the symbolic in a new synthesis. They know that neither science nor sociology can be rejected. They know, too, that they cannot become the slaves of either of these. The dilemma, in another form, has been faced successfully before, and it can be again. And the synthesis may be broadened to include the integration of conscious and unconscious experience, of man and machine, but above all the creative individual life balanced with the constant effort to help shape the face of the world in which the poet, like everyone else, must live.

Poetry is the greatest of the arts because everyone can —and does—practise it. The ad-man and the gag-man, the housewife and the corner-grocer are latent poets. Especially is the poetry of Carl Sandburg great for this reason. Not because it gives words and ideas memorable form (it rarely does); but because it captures and records lovingly the poetry in the common speech, attitudes and aspirations of the people. That is why we have the paradox of the most original and indigenous

American art in the anonymous outpourings of the oppressed Negro. That is why I have included the words of some of their songs. And that is why I have included the last speech of Vanzetti, eloquent with compassion and anguish, which falls into lines as easily as the frost into crystals.

PART ONE

Poetry

I too, dislike it: there are things that are important
beyond all this fiddle.
Reading it, however, with a perfect contempt for it,
one discovers in
it after all, a place for the genuine.
Hands that can grasp, eyes
that can dilate, hair that can rise
if it must, these things are important not because a

high sounding interpretation can be put upon them
but because they are
useful. When they become so derivative
as to become unintelligible,
the same thing may be said for all of us, that we
do not admire what
we cannot understand: the bat,
holding on upside down or in quest of something to

eat, elephants pushing, a wild horse taking a roll,
a tireless wolf under
a tree, the immovable critic twitching his skin
like a horse that feels a flea, the base-
ball fan, the statistician—
nor is it valid
to discriminate against 'business documents and

school-books'; all these phenomena are important.
One must make a distinction

however: when dragged into prominence by half-poets,
the result is not poetry,
nor till the poets among us can be
'literalists of
the imagination'—above
insolence and triviality and can present

for inspection, imaginary gardens with real toads in
them, shall we have
it. In the meantime, if you demand on the one hand,
the raw material of poetry in
all its rawness and
that which is on the other hand
genuine, then you are interested in poetry.

—Marianne Moore

Afterwards

THOMAS HARDY

When the Present has latched its postern behind my
tremulous stay,
And the May month flaps its glad green leaves like
wings,
Delicate-filmed as new-spun silk, will the neighbors say,
"He was a man who used to notice such things"?

If it be in the dusk when, like an eyelid's soundless
blink,
The dewfall-hawk comes crossing the shades to alight
Upon the wind-warped upland thorn, a gazer may think,
"To him this must have been a familiar sight."

If I pass during some nocturnal blackness, mothy and
warm,
When the hedgehog travels furtively over the lawn,
One may say, "He strove that such innocent creatures
should come to no harm,
But he could do little for them; and now he is gone."

If, when hearing that I have been stilled at last, they
stand at the door,
Watching the full-starred heavens that winter sees,
Will this thought rise on those who will meet my face
no more,
"He was one who had an eye for such mysteries?"

And will any say when my bell of quittance is heard in
the gloom,
And a crossing breeze cuts a pause in its out-rollings,
Till they rise again, as they were a new bell's boom,
"He hears it not now, but used to notice such things?"

Jabberwocky

LEWIS CARROLL

'Twas brillig, and the slithy toves
  Did gyre and gimble in the wabe;
All mimsy were the borogoves,
  And the mome raths outgrabe.

"Beware the Jabberwock, my son!
  The jaws that bite, the claws that catch!
Beware the Jubjub bird, and shun
  The frumious Bandersnatch!"

He took his vorpal sword in hand:
  Long time the manxome foe he sought—
So rested he by the Tumtum tree,
  And stood awhile in thought.

And as in uffish thought he stood,
  The Jabberwock with eyes of flame,
Came whiffling through the tulgey wood,
  And burbled as it came!

One, two! One, two! And through and through
  The vorpal blade went snicker-snack!
He left it dead, and with its head
  He went galumphing back.

"And hast thou slain the Jabberwock?
Come to my arms, my beamish boy!
O frabjous day! Callooh! Callay!"
He chortled in his joy.

'Twas brillig, and the slithy toves
Did gyre and gimble in the wabe;
All mimsy were the borogoves,
And the mome raths outgrabe.

From *Reynard the Fox*

JOHN MASEFIELD

From the Gallows Hill to the Tineton Copse
There were ten ploughed fields, like ten full-stops,
All wet red clay, where a horse's foot
Would be swathed, feet thick, like an ash-tree root.
The fox raced on, on the headlands firm,
Where his swift feet scared the coupling worm;
The rooks rose raving to curse him raw,
He snarled a sneer at their swoop and caw.
Then on, then on, down a half-ploughed field
Where a ship-like plough drove glitter-keeled,
With a bay horse near and a white horse leading,
And a man saying "Zook," and the red earth bleeding.
He gasped as he saw the ploughman drop
The stilts and swear at the team to stop.
The ploughman ran in his red clay clogs,
Crying, "Zick un, Towzer; zick, good dogs!"
A couple of wire-haired lurchers lean
Arose from his wallet, nosing keen;
With a rushing swoop they were on his track,
Putting chest to stubble to bite his back.
He swerved from his line with the curs at heel,
The teeth as they missed him clicked like steel.
With a worrying snarl, they quartered on him,
While the ploughman shouted, "Zick; upon him."

*

The fox raced on, up the Barton Balks,
With a crackle of kex in the nettle stalks,
Over Hammond's grass to the dark green line
Of the larch-wood smelling of turpentine.
Scratch Steven Larches, black to the sky,
A sadness breathing with one long sigh,
Grey ghosts of trees under funeral plumes,
A mist of twig over soft brown glooms.
As he entered the wood he heard the smacks,
Chip-jar, of the fir-pole feller's axe.
He swerved to the left to a broad green ride,
Where a boy made him rush for the farther side.
He swerved to the left, to the Barton Road,
But there were the timberers come to load—
Two timber carts and a couple of carters
With straps round their knees instead of garters.
He swerved to the right, straight down the wood,
The carters watched him, the boy hallooed.
He leaped from the larch-wood into tillage,
The cobbler's garden of Barton village.

*

The cobbler bent at his wooden foot,
Beating sprigs in a broken boot;
He wore old glasses with thick horn rim,
He scowled at his work for his sight was dim.
His face was dingy, his lips were grey,
From primming sparrowbills day by day.
As he turned his boot he heard a noise
At his garden-end, and he thought, "It's boys."

Like a rocket shot to a ship ashore
The lean red bolt of his body tore,
Like a ripple of wind running swift on grass;
Like a shadow on wheat when a cloud blows past,
Like a turn at the buoy in a cutter sailing
When the bright green gleam lips white at the railing,
Like the April snake whipping back to sheath,
Like the gannets' hurtle on fish beneath,
Like a kestrel chasing, like a sickle reaping,
Like all things swooping, like all things sweeping,
Like a hound for stay, like a stag for swift,
With his shadow beside like spinning drift.

*

Past the gibbet-stock all stuck with nails,
Where they hanged in chains what had hung at jails,
Past Ashmundshowe where Ashmund sleeps,
And none but the tumbling peewit weeps,
Past Curlew Calling, the gaunt grey corner
Where the curlew comes as a summer mourner,
Past Blowbury Beacon, shaking his fleece,
Where all winds hurry and none brings peace;
Then down on the mile-long green decline,
Where the turf's like spring and the air's like wine,
Where the sweeping spurs of the downland spill
Into Wan Brook Valley and Wan Dyke Hill.

*

On he went with a galloping rally
Past Maesbury Clump for Wan Brook Valley.

The blood in his veins went romping high,
"Get on, on, on, to the earth or die."
The air of the downs went purely past
Till he felt the glory of going fast,
Till the terror of death, though there indeed,
Was lulled for a while by his pride of speed.
He was romping away from the hounds and hunt,
He had Wan Dyke Hill and his earth in front,
In a one mile more when his point was made
He would rest in safety from dog or spade;
Nose between paws he would hear the shout
Of the "Gone to earth!" to the hounds without,
The whine of the hounds, and their cat-feet gadding
Scratching the earth, and their breath pad-padding;
He would hear the horn call hounds away,
And rest in peace till another day.

Others, I am not the first

A. E. HOUSMAN

Others, I am not the first,
Have willed more mischief than they durst:
If in the breathless night I too
Shiver now, 'tis nothing new.

More than I, if truth were told,
Have stood and sweated hot and cold,
And through their reins in ice and fire
Fear contended with desire.

Agued once like me were they,
But I like them shall win my way
Lastly to the bed of mould
Where there's neither heat nor cold.

But from my grave across my brow
Plays no wind of healing now,
And fire and ice within me fight
Beneath the suffocating night.

1887

A. E. HOUSMAN

From Clee to heaven the beacon burns,
  The shires have seen it plain,
From north and south the sign returns
  And beacons burn again.

Look left, look right, the hills are bright,
  The dales are light between,
Because 'tis fifty years tonight
  That God has saved the Queen.

Now, when the flame they watch not towers
  Above the soil they trod,
Lads, we'll remember friends of ours
  Who shared the work with God.

To skies that knit their heartstrings right,
  To fields that bred them brave,
The saviours come not home tonight:
  Themselves they could not save.

It dawns in Asia, tombstones show
  And Shropshire names are read;
And the Nile spills his overflow
  Beside the Severn's dead.

We pledge in peace by farm and town
  The Queen they served in war,
And fire the beacons up and down
  The land they perished for.

'God save the Queen' we living sing,
  From height to height 'tis heard;
And with the rest your voices ring,
  Lads of the Fifty-third.

Oh, God will save her, fear you not:
  Be you the men you've been,
Get you the sons your fathers got,
  And God will save the Queen.

Terence, this is stupid stuff

A. E. HOUSMAN

'Terence, this is stupid stuff:
You eat your victuals fast enough;
There can't be much amiss, 'tis clear,
To see the rate you drink your beer.
But oh, good Lord, the verse you make,
It gives a chap the belly-ache.
The cow, the old cow, she is dead;
It sleeps well, the horned head:
We poor lads, 'tis our turn now
To hear such tunes as killed the cow.
Pretty friendship 'tis to rhyme
Your friends to death before their time
Moping melancholy mad:
Come, pipe a tune to dance to, lad.'

Why, if 'tis dancing you would be,
There's brisker pipes than poetry.
Say, for what were hop-yards meant,
Or why was Burton built on Trent?
Oh many a peer of England brews
Livelier liquor than the Muse,
And malt does more than Milton can
To justify God's ways to man.
Ale, man, ale's the stuff to drink
For fellows whom it hurts to think:

Look into the pewter pot
To see the world as the world's not.
And faith, 'tis pleasant till 'tis past:
The mischief is that 'twill not last.
Oh I have been to Ludlow fair
And left my necktie God knows where,
And carried half way home, or near,
Pints and quarts of Ludlow beer:
Then the world seemed none so bad,
And I myself a sterling lad;
And down in lovely muck I've lain,
Happy till I woke again.
Then I saw the morning sky:
Heigho, the tale was all a lie;
The world, it was the old world yet,
I was I, my things were wet,
And nothing now remained to do
But begin the game anew.

Therefore, since the world has still
Much good, but much less good than ill,
And while the sun and moon endure
Luck's a chance, but trouble's sure,
I'd face it as a wise man would,
And train for ill and not for good.
'Tis true, the stuff I bring for sale
Is not so brisk a brew as ale:
Out of a stem that scored the hand
I wrung it in a weary land.

But take it: if the smack is sour,
The better for the embittered hour;
It should do good to heart and head
When your soul is in my soul's stead;
And I will friend you, if I may
In the dark and cloudy day.

There was a king reigned in the East:
There, when kings will sit to feast,
They get their fill before they think
With poisoned meat and poisoned drink.
He gathered all that springs to birth
From the many-venomed earth;
First a little, thence to more,
He sampled all her killing store;
And easy, smiling, seasoned sound,
Sate the king when healths went round.
They put arsenic in his meat
And stared aghast to watch him eat;
They poured strychnine in his cup
And shook to see him drink it up:
They shook, they stared as white's their shirt;
Them it was their poison hurt.
—I tell the tale that I heard told.
Mithridates, he died old.

The Listeners

WALTER DE LA MARE

'Is there anybody there?' said the Traveller,
  Knocking on the moonlit door;
And his horse in the silence champed the grasses
  Of the forest's ferny floor:
And a bird flew up out of a turret,
  Above the Traveller's head:
And he smote upon the door again a second time;
  'Is there anybody there?' he said.
But no one descended to the Traveller;
  No head from the leaf-fringed sill
Leaned over and looked into his grey eyes,
  Where he stood perplexed and still.
But only a host of phantom listeners
  That dwelt in the lone house then
Stood listening in the quiet of the moonlight
  To that voice from the world of men:
Stood thronging the faint moonbeams on the dark stair,
  That goes down to the empty hall,
Hearkening in an air stirred and shaken
  By the lonely Traveller's call.
And he felt in his heart their strangeness,
  Their stillness answering his cry,
While his horse moved, cropping the dark turf,
  'Neath the starred and leafy sky;

For he suddenly smote on the door, even
  Louder, and lifted his head:—
'Tell them I came, and no one answered,
  That I kept my word,' he said.
Never the least stir made the listeners,
  Though every word he spake
Fell echoing through the shadowiness of the still house
  From the one man left awake:
Aye, they heard his foot upon the stirrup,
  And the sound of iron on stone,
And how the silence surged softly backward,
  When the plunging hoofs were gone.

Johannes Milton, Senex

ROBERT BRIDGES

Since I believe in God the Father Almighty
Man's Maker and Judge, Overruler of Fortune,
'Twere strange should I praise anything and refuse Him
  praise,
Should love the creature forgetting the Creator,
Nor unto Him in suff'ring and sorrow turn me:
Nay how cou'd I withdraw me from His embracing?

But since that I have seen not, and cannot know Him,
Nor in my earthly temple apprehend rightly
His wisdom and the heav'nly purpose eternal;
Therefore will I be bound to no studied system
Nor argument, nor with delusion enslave me,
Nor seek to please Him in any foolish invention
Which my spirit within me, that loveth beauty
And hateth evil, hath reprov'd as unworthy:

But I cherish my freedom in loving service,
Gratefully adoring for delight beyond asking
Or thinking, and in hours of anguish and darkness
Confiding always on His excellent greatness.

From *The Great Lover*

RUPERT BROOKE

These I have loved:
White plates and cups, clean-gleaming,
Ringed with blue lines; and feathery, faery dust;
Wet roofs, beneath the lamp-light; the strong crust
Of friendly bread; and many-tasting food;
Rainbows; and the blue bitter smoke of wood;
And radiant raindrops couching in cool flowers;
And flowers themselves, that sway through sunny hours,
Dreaming of moths that drink them under the moon;
Then, the cool kindliness of sheets, that soon
Smooth away trouble; and the rough male kiss
Of blankets; grainy wood; live hair that is
Shining and free; blue-massing clouds; the keen
Unpassioned beauty of a great machine;
The benison of hot water; furs to touch;
The good smell of old clothes; and other such–
The comfortable smell of friendly fingers,
Hair's fragrance, and the musty reek that lingers
About dead leaves and last year's ferns. . . .

Wagner

RUPERT BROOKE

Creeps in half wanton, half asleep,
  One with a fat wide hairless face.
He likes love-music that is cheap;
  Likes women in a crowded place;
    And wants to hear the noise they're making.

His heavy eyelids droop half-over,
  Great pouches swing beneath his eyes.
He listens, thinks himself the lover,
  Heaves from his stomach wheezy sighs;
    He likes to feel his heart's a-breaking.

The music swells. His gross legs quiver.
  His little lips are bright with slime.
The music swells. The women shiver.
  And all the while, in perfect time,
    His pendulous stomach hangs a-shaking.

Wild Peaches

ELINOR WYLIE

1.

When the world turns completely upside down
You say we'll emigrate to the Eastern Shore
Aboard a river-boat from Baltimore;
We'll live among wild peach trees, miles from town,
You'll wear a coonskin cap, and I a gown
Homespun, dyed butternut's dark gold colour.
Lost, like your lotus-eating ancestor,
We'll swim in milk and honey till we drown.

The winter will be short, the summer long,
The autumn amber-hued, sunny and hot,
Tasting of cider and of scuppernong;
All seasons sweet, but autumn best of all.
The squirrels in their silver fur will fall
Like falling leaves, like fruit, before your shot.

2.

The autumn frosts will lie upon the grass
Like bloom on grapes of purple-brown and gold.
The misted early mornings will be cold;
The little puddles will be roofed with glass.
The sun, which burns from copper into brass,
Melts these at noon, and makes the boys unfold
Their knitted mufflers; full as they can hold,
Fat pockets dribble chestnuts as they pass.

Peaches grow wild, and pigs can live in clover;
A barrel of salted herrings lasts a year;
The spring begins before the winter's over.
By February you may find the skins
Of garter snakes and water moccasins
Dwindled and harsh, dead-white and cloudy-clear.

3.

When April pours the colours of a shell
Upon the hills, when every little creek
Is shot with silver from the Chesapeake
In shoals new-minted by the ocean swell,
When strawberries go begging, and the sleek
Blue plums lie open to the blackbird's beak,
We shall live well—we shall live very well.

The months between the cherries and the peaches
Are brimming cornucopias which spill
Fruits red and purple, sombre-bloomed and black;
Then, down rich fields and frosty river beaches
We'll trample bright persimmons, while you kill
Bronze partridge, speckled quail, and canvasback.

4.

Down to the Puritan marrow of my bones
There's something in this richness that I hate.
I love the look, austere, immaculate,
Of landscapes drawn in pearly monotones.
There's something in my very blood that owns

Bare hills, cold silver on a sky of slate,
A thread of water, churned to milky spate
Streaming through slanted pastures fenced with stones.

I love those skies, thin blue or snowy gray
Those fields sparse-planted, rendering meagre sheaves;
That spring, briefer than apple-blossom's breath,
Summer, so much too beautiful to stay,
Swift autumn, like a bonfire of leaves,
And sleepy winter, like the sleep of death.

Castilian

ELINOR WYLIE

Velasquez took a pliant knife
And scraped his palette clean;
He said, "I lead a dog's own life
Painting a king and queen."

He cleaned his palette with oily rags
And oakum from Seville wharves;
"I am sick of painting painted hags
And bad ambiguous dwarves.

"The sky is silver, the clouds are pearl,
Their locks are looped with rain.
I will not paint Maria's girl
For all the money in Spain."

He washed his face in water cold,
His hands in turpentine;
He squeezed out colour like coins of gold
And colour like drops of wine.

Each colour lay like a little pool
On the polished cedar wood;
Clear and pale and ivory-cool
Or dark as solitude.

He burnt the rags in the fireplace
And leaned from the window high;
He said, "I like that gentleman's face
Who wears his cap awry."

This is the gentleman, there he stands,
Castilian, sombre-caped,
With arrogant eyes, and narrow hands
Miraculously shaped.

Moriturus

EDNA ST. VINCENT MILLAY

If I could have
  Two things in one:
The peace of the grave,
  And the light of the sun;

My hands across
  My thin breast-bone,
But aware of the moss
  Invading the stone,

Aware of the flight
  Of the golden flicker
With his wing to the light;
  To hear him nicker

And drum with his bill
  On the rotted window;
Snug and still
  On a gray pillow

Deep in the clay
  Where digging is hard,
Out of the way,—
  The blue shard

Of a broken platter—
  If I might be
Insensate matter
  With sensate me

Sitting within,
  Harking and prying,
I might begin
  To dicker with dying.

For the body at best
  Is a bundle of aches,
Longing for rest;
  It cries when it wakes

"Alas, 'tis light!"
  At set of sun
"Alas, 'tis night,
  And nothing done!"

Death, however,
  Is a spongy wall,
Is a sticky river,
  Is nothing at all.

Summon the weeper,
  Wail and sing;
Call him Reaper,
  Angel, King;

Call him Evil
  Drunk to the lees,
Monster, Devil,—
  He is less than these.

Call him Thief,
  The Maggot in the Cheese,
The Canker in the Leaf—
  He is less than these.

Dusk without sound,
  Where the spirit by pain
Uncoiled, is wound
  To spring again;

The mind enmeshed
  Laid straight in repose,
And the body refreshed
  By feeding the rose—

These are but visions;
  These would be
The grave's derisions,
  Could the grave see.

Here is the wish
  Of one that died
Like a beached fish
  On the ebb of the tide:

That he might wait
  Till the tide came back,
To see if a crate,
  Or a bottle, or a black

Boot, or an oar,
  Or an orange peel
Be washed ashore. . . .
  About his heel

The sand slips;
  The last he hears
From the world's lips
  Is the sand in his ears.

What thing is little?—
  The aphis hid
In a house of spittle?
  The hinge of the lid

Of the spider's eye
  At the spider's birth?
"Greater am I
  By the earth's girth

"Than Mighty Death!"
  All creatures cry
That can summon breath—
  And speak no lie.

For he is nothing;
  He is less
Than Echo answering
  "Nothingness!"—

Less than the heat
  Of the furthest star
To the ripening wheat;
  Less by far,

When all the lipping
  Is said and sung,
Than the sweat dripping
  From a dog's tongue.

This being so,
  And I being such,
I would liever go
  On a cripple's crutch,

Lopped and felled;
  Liever be dependent
On a chair propelled
  By a surly attendant

With a foul breath,
  And be spooned my food,
Than go with Death
  Where nothing good,

Not even the thrust
  Of the summer gnat,
Consoles the dust
  For being that.

Needy, lonely,
  Stitched by pain,
Left with only
  The drip of the rain

Out of all I had;
  The books of the wise,
Badly read
  By other eyes,

Lewdly bawled
  At my closing ear;
Hated, called
  A lingerer here—

Withstanding Death
  Till Life be gone,
I shall treasure my breath,
  I shall linger on.

I shall bolt my door
  With a bolt and a cable;
I shall block my door
  With a bureau and a table;

With all my might
  My door shall be barred.
I shall put up a fight,
  I shall take it hard.

With his hand on my mouth
  He shall drag me forth,
Shrieking to the south
  And clutching at the north.

Practical People

ROBINSON JEFFERS

Practical people, I have been told,
Weary of the sea for his waves go up and down
Endlessly to no visible purpose;
Tire of the tides, for the tides are tireless, the tides
Are well content with their own march-tune
And nothing accomplished is no matter to them.
It seems wasteful to practical people.
And that the nations labor and gather and dissolve
Into destruction; the stars sharpen
Their spirit of splendor, and then it dims, and the stars
Darken; and that the spirit of man
Sharpens up to maturity and cools dull
With age, dies, and rusts out of service;
And all these tidal gatherings, growth and decay,
Shining and darkening, are forever
Renewed; and the whole cycle impenitently
Revolves, and all the past is future:—
Make it a difficult world . . . for practical people.

Shine, Perishing Republic

ROBINSON JEFFERS

While this America settles in the mould of its vulgarity,
heavily thickening to empire,
And protest, only a bubble in the molten mass, pops and
sighs out, and the mass hardens,

I sadly remember that the flower fades to make fruit,
the fruit rots to make earth.
Out of the mother; and through the spring exultances,
ripeness and decadence; and home to the mother.

You making haste haste on decay: not blameworthy;
life is
good, be it stubbornly long or suddenly
A mortal splendor: meteors are not needed less than
mountains: shine, perishing republic.

But for my children, I would rather have them keep
their distance
from the thickening center; corruption
Never has been compulsory, when the cities lie at the
monster's feet there are left the mountains.

And boys, be in nothing so moderate as in love of man, a
clever servant, insufferable master.
There is the trap that catches noblest spirits, that caught—
they say—God, when he walked on earth.

Roan Stallion

ROBINSON JEFFERS

The dog barked; then the woman stood in the doorway, and hearing iron strike stone down the steep road
Covered her head with a black shawl and entered the light rain; she stood at the turn of the road.
A nobly formed woman; erect and strong as a new tower; the features stolid and dark
But sculptured into a strong grace; straight nose with a high bridge, firm and wide eyes, full chin,
Red lips; she was only a fourth part Indian; a Scottish sailor had planted her in young native earth,
Spanish and Indian, twenty-one years before. He had named her California when she was born;
That was her name; and had gone north.
She heard the hooves and wheels come nearer, up the steep road.
The buckskin mare, leaning against the breastpiece, plodded into sight round the wet bank.
The pale face of the driver followed; the burnt-out eyes; they had fortune in them. He sat twisted
On the seat of the old buggy, leading a second horse by a long halter, a roan, a big one,
That stepped daintily; by the swell of the neck, a stallion. "What have you got, Johnny?" "Maskerel's stallion.

Mine now. I won him last night, I had very good luck."
He was quite drunk. "They bring their mares up here now.
I keep this fellow. I got money besides, but I'll not show you." "Did you buy something, Johnny,
For our Christine? Christmas comes in two days, Johnny." "By God, forgot," he answered laughing.
"Don't tell Christine it's Christmas; after while I get her something, maybe." But California:
"I shared your luck when you lost: you lost *me* once, Johnny, remember? Tom Dell had me two nights
Here in the house: other times we've gone hungry: now that you've won, Christine will have her Christmas.
We share your luck, Johnny. You give me money, I go down to Monterey to-morrow,
Buy presents for Christine, come back in the evening. Next day Christmas." "You have wet ride," he answered
Giggling. "Here money. Five dollar; ten; twelve dollar. You buy two bottles of rye whisky for Johnny."
"All right. I go to-morrow."

He was an outcast Hollander; not old, but shriveled with bad living.
The child Christine inherited from his race blue eyes, from his life a wizened forehead; she watched
From the house-door her father lurch out of the buggy and lead with due respect the stallion
To the new corral, the strong one; leaving the wearily breathing buckskin mare to his wife to unharness.

Storm in the night; the rain on the thin shakes of the roof like the ocean on rock streamed battering; once thunder
Walked down the narrow canyon into Carmel valley and wore away westward; Christine was wakeful
With fears and wonders; her father lay too deep for storm to touch him.
Dawn comes late in the year's dark,
Later into the crack of a canyon under redwoods; and California slipped from bed
An hour before it; the buckskin would be tired; there was a little barley, and why should Johnny
Feed all the barley to his stallion? That is what he would do. She tiptoed out of the room.
Leaving her clothes, he'd waken if she waited to put them on, and passed from the door of the house
Into the dark of the rain; the big black drops were cold through the thin shift, but the wet earth
Pleasant under her naked feet. There was a pleasant smell in the stable; and moving softly,
Touching things gently with the supple bend of the unclothed body, was pleasant. She found a box,
Filled it with sweet dry barley and took it down to the old corral. The little mare sighed deeply
At the rail in the wet darkness; and California returning between two redwoods up to the house
Heard the happy jaws grinding the grain. Johnny could mind the pigs and chickens. Christine called to her

When she entered the house, but slept again under her hand. She laid the wet night-dress on a chair-back
And stole into the bedroom to get her clothes. A plank creaked, and he wakened. She stood motionless
Hearing him stir in the bed. When he was quiet she stooped after her shoes, and he said softly,
"What are you doing? Come back to bed." "It's late, I'm going to Monterey, I must hitch up."
"You come to bed first. I been away three days. I give you money, I take back the money
And what you do in town then?" She sighed sharply and came to the bed.

He reaching his hands from it
Felt the cool curve and firmness of her flank, and half rising caught her by the long wet hair.
She endured, and to hasten the act she feigned desire; she had not for long, except in dream, felt it.
Yesterday's drunkenness made him sluggish and exacting; she saw, turning her head sadly,
The windows were bright gray with dawn; he embraced her still, stopping to talk about the stallion.
At length she was permitted to put on her clothes. Clear daylight over the steep hills;
Gray-shining cloud over the tops of the redwoods; the winter stream sang loud; the wheels of the buggy
Slipped in deep slime, ground on washed stones at the roadedge. Down the hill the wrinkled river smothered the ford.

You must keep to the bed of stones: she knew the way by willow and alder: the buckskin halted midstream,
Shuddering, the water her own color washing up to the traces; but California, drawing up
Her feet out of the whirl onto the seat of the buggy swung the whip over the yellow water
And drove to the road.

All morning the clouds were racing northward like a river. At noon they thickened.
When California faced the southwind home from Monterey it was heavy with level rainfall.
She looked seaward from the foot of the valley; red rays cried sunset from a trumpet of streaming
Cloud over Lobos, the southwest occident of the solstice. Twilight came soon, but the tired mare
Feared the road more than the whip. Mile after mile of slow gray twilight.

Then, quite suddenly, darkness.
"Christine will be asleep. It is Christmas Eve. The ford. That hour of daylight wasted this morning!"
She could see nothing; she let the reins lie on the dashboard and knew at length by the cramp of the wheels
And the pitch down, they had reached it. Noise of wheels on stones, plashing of hooves in water; a world
Of sounds; no sight; the gentle thunder of water; the mare snorting, dipping her head, one knew,

To look for footing, in the blackness, under the stream.
The hushing and creaking of the sea-wind
In the passion of invisible willows.
The mare stood still; the woman shouted to her; spared whip,
For a false leap would lose the track of the ford. She stood. "The baby's things," thought California,
"Under the seat: the water will come over the floor"; and rising in the midst of the water
She tilted the seat; fetched up the doll, the painted wooden chickens, the woolly bear, the book
Of many pictures, the box of sweets: she brought them all from under the seat and stored them, trembling,
Under her clothes, about the breasts, under the arms; the corners of the cardboard boxes
Cut into the soft flesh; but with a piece of rope for a girdle and wound about the shoulders
All was made fast. The mare stood still as if asleep in the midst of the water. Then California
Reached out a hand over the stream and fingered her rump; the solid wet convexity of it
Shook like the beat of a great heart. "What are you waiting for?" But the feel of the animal surface
Had wakened a dream, obscured real danger with a dream of danger. "What for? for the water-stallion
To break out of the stream, that is what the rump strains for, him to come up flinging foam sidewise,
Fore-hooves in air, crush me and the rig and curl over his woman." She flung out with the whip then;

The mare plunged forward. The buggy drifted sidelong:
was she off ground? Swimming? No: by the splashes.
The driver, a mere prehensile instinct, clung to the
sideirons of the seat and felt the force
But not the coldness of the water, curling over her
knees, breaking up to the waist
Over her body. They'd turned. The mare had turned
up stream and was wallowing back into shoal
water.
Then California dropped her forehead to her knees,
having seen nothing, feeling a danger,
And felt the brute weight of a branch of alder, the
pendulous light leaves brush her bent neck
Like a child's fingers. The mare burst out of water and
stopped on the slope to the ford. The woman
climbed down
Between the wheels and went to her head. "Poor Dora,"
she called her by her name, "there, Dora. Quietly,"
And led her around, there was room to turn on the
margin, the head to the gentle thunder of the
water.
She crawled on hands and knees, felt for the ruts, and
shifted the wheels into them. "You can see, Dora.
I can't. But this time you'll go through it." She climbed
into the seat and shouted angrily. The mare
Stopped, her two forefeet in the water. She touched
with the whip. The mare plodded ahead and halted.
Then California thought of prayer: "Dear little Jesus,
Dear baby Jesus born to-night, your head was shining

Like silver candles. I've got a baby too, only a girl. You had light wherever you walked.
Dear baby Jesus give me light." Light streamed: rose, gold, rich purple, hiding the ford like a curtain.
The gentle thunder of water was a noise of wing-feathers, the fans of paradise lifting softly.
The child afloat on radiance had a baby face, but the angels had birds' heads, hawks' heads,
Bending over the baby, weaving a web of wings about him. He held in the small fat hand
A little snake with golden eyes, and California could see clearly on the under radiance
The mare's pricked ears, a sharp black fork against the shining light-fall. But it dropped; the light of heaven
Frightened poor Dora. She backed; swung up the water,
And nearly oversetting the buggy turned and scrambled backward; the iron wheel-tires rang on boulders.

Then California weeping climbed between the wheels. Her wet clothes and the toys packed under
Dragged her down with their weight; she stripped off cloak and dress and laid the baby's things in the buggy;
Brought Johnny's whisky out from under the seat; wrapped all in the dress, bottles and toys, and tied them
Into a bundle that would sling over her back. She unharnessed the mare, hurting her fingers

Against the swollen straps and the wet buckles. She tied the pack over her shoulders, the cords
Crossing her breasts, and mounted. She drew up her shift about her waist and knotted it, naked thighs
Clutching the sides of the mare, bare flesh to the wet withers, and caught the mane with her right hand,
The looped-up bridle-reins in the other. "Dora, the baby gives you light." The blinding radiance
Hovered the ford. "Sweet baby Jesus give us light." Cataracts of light and Latin singing
Fell through the willows; the mare snorted and reared: the roar and thunder of the invisible water;
The night shaking open like a flag, shot with the flashes; the baby face hovering; the water
Beating over her shoes and stockings up to the bare thighs; and over them, like a beast
Lapping her belly; the wriggle and pitch of the mare swimming; the drift, the sucking water; the blinding
Light above and behind with not a gleam before, in the throat of darkness; the shock of the fore-hooves
Striking bottom, the struggle and surging lift of the haunches. She felt the water streaming off her
From the shoulders down; heard the great strain and sob of the mare's breathing, heard the horseshoes grind on gravel.
When California came home the dog at the door snuffed at her without barking; Christine and Johnny

Both were asleep; she did not sleep for hours, but kindled fire and knelt patiently over it,
Shaping and drying the dear-bought gifts for Christmas morning.

She hated (she thought) the proud-necked stallion.
He'd lean the big twin masses of his breast on the rail, his red-brown eyes flash the white crescents,
She admired him then, she hated him for his uselessness, serving nothing
But Johnny's vanity. Horses were too cheap to breed. She thought, if he could range in freedom,
Shaking the red-roan mane for a flag on the bare hills.

A man brought up a mare in April;
Then California, though she wanted to watch, stayed with Christine indoors. When the child fretted
The mother told her once more about the miracle of the ford; her prayers to the little Jesus
The Christmas Eve when she was bringing the gifts home; the appearance, the lights, the Latin singing,
The thunder of wing-feathers and water, the shining child, the cataracts of splendor down the darkness.
"A little baby," Christine asked, "the God is a baby?" "The child of God. That was his birthday.
His mother was named Mary: we pray to her too: God came to her. He was not the child of a man
Like you or me. God was his father: she was the stallion's wife—what did I say—God's wife,"

She said with a cry, lifting Christine aside, pacing the planks of the floor. "She is called more blessed
Than any woman. She was so good, she was more loved."
"Did God live near her house?" "He lives
Up high, over the stars; he ranges on the bare blue hill of the sky." In her mind a picture
Flashed, of the red-roan mare shaken out for a flag on the bare hills, and she said quickly, "He's more
Like a great man holding the sun in his hand." Her mind giving her words the lie, "But no one
Knows, only the shining and the power. The power, the terror, the burning fire covered her over . . ."
"Was she burnt up, mother?" "She was so good and lovely, she was the mother of the little Jesus.
If you are good nothing will hurt you." "What did she think?" "She loved, she was not afraid of the hooves—
Hands that had made the hills and sun and moon, and the sea and the great redwoods, the terrible strength,
She gave herself without thinking." "You only saw the baby, mother?" "Yes, and the angels about him,
The great wild shining over the black river." Three times she had walked to the door, three times returned,
And now the hand that had thrice hung on the knob, full of prevented action, twisted the cloth
Of the child's dress that she had been mending. "Oh,

Oh, I've torn it." She struck at the child and then embraced her
Fiercely, the small blond sickly body.
Johnny came in, his face reddened as if he had stood
Near fire, his eyes triumphing. "Finished," he said, and looked with malice at Christine. "I go
Down valley with Jim Carrier; owes me five dollar, fifteen I charge him, he brought ten in his pocket.
Has grapes on the ranch, maybe I take a barrel red wine instead of money. Be back to-morrow.
To-morrow night I tell you—Eh, Jim," he laughed over his shoulder, "I say to-morrow evening
I show her how the red fellow act, the big fellow. When I come home." She answered nothing, but stood
In front of the door, holding the little hand of her daughter, in the path of sun between the redwoods,
While Johnny tied the buckskin mare behind Carrier's buggy, and bringing saddle and bridle tossed them
Under the seat. Jim Carrier's mare, the bay, stood with drooped head and started slowly, the men
Laughing and shouting at her; their voices could be heard down the steep road, after the noise
Of the iron-hooped wheels died from the stone. Then one might hear the hush of the wind in the tall redwoods,
The tinkle of the April brook, deep in its hollow.
Humanity is the start of the race; I say

Humanity is the mold to break away from, the crust to
break through, the coal to break into fire,
The atom to be split.
Tragedy that breaks man's face and a
white fire flies out of it; vision that fools him
Out of his limits, desire that fools him out of his limits,
unnatural crime, inhuman science,
Slit eyes in the mask; wild loves that leap over the walls
of nature, the wild fence-vaulter science,
Useless intelligence of far stars, dim knowledge of the
spinning demons that make an atom,
These break, these pierce, these deify, praising their God
shrilly with fierce voices: not in man's shape
He approves the praise, he that walks lightning-naked
on the Pacific, that laces the suns with planets,
The heart of the atom with electrons: what is humanity
in this cosmos? For him, the last
Least taint of a trace in the dregs of the solution; for
itself, the mold to break away from, the coal
To break into fire, the atom to be split.

After the child slept, after
the leopard-footed evening
Had glided oceanward, California turned the lamp to its
least flame and glided from the house.
She moved sighing, like a loose fire, backward and
forward on the smooth ground by the door.
She heard the night-wind that draws down the valley
like the draught in a flue under clear weather

Whisper and toss in the tall redwoods; she heard the tinkle of the April brook deep in its hollow.
Cooled by the night the odors that the horses had left behind were in her nostrils; the night
Whitened up the bare hill; a drift of coyotes by the river cried bitterly against moonrise;
Then California ran to the old corral, the empty one where they kept the buckskin mare,
And leaned, and bruised her breasts on the rail, feeling the sky whiten. When the moon stood over the hill
She stole to the house. The child breathed quietly. Herself: to sleep? She had seen Christ in the night at Christmas.
The hills were shining open to the enormous night of the April moon: empty and empty,
The vast round backs of the bare hills? If one should ride up high might not the Father himself
Be seen brooding His night, cross-legged, chin in hand, squatting on the last dome? More likely
Leaping the hills, shaking the red-roan mane for a flag on the bare hills. She blew out the lamp.
Every fiber of flesh trembled with faintness when she came to the door; strength lacked, to wander
Afoot into the shining of the hill, high enough, high enough . . . the hateful face of a man had taken
The strength that might have served her, the corral was empty. The dog followed her, she caught him by the collar,

Dragged him in fierce silence back to the door of the house, latched him inside.

It was like daylight

Out-doors and she hastened without faltering down the footpath, through the dark fringe of twisted oak-brush,

To the open place in a bay of the hill. The dark strength of the stallion had heard her coming; she heard him

Blow the shining air out of his nostrils, she saw him in the white lake of moonlight

Move like a lion along the timbers of the fence, shaking the nightfall

Of the great mane; his fragrance came to her; she leaned on the fence;

He drew away from it, the hooves making soft thunder in the trodden soil.

Wild love had trodden it, his wrestling with the stranger, the shame of the day

Had stamped it into mire and powder when the heavy fetlocks

Strained the soft flanks. "Oh, if I could bear you!

If I had the strength. O great God that came down to Mary, gently you came. But I will ride him

Up into the hill, if he throws me, if he tramples me, is it not my desire

To endure death?" She climbed the fence, pressing her body against the rail, shaking like fever,

And dropped inside to the soft ground. He neither

threatened her with his teeth nor fled from her coming,
And lifting her hand gently to the upflung head she caught the strap of the headstall,
That hung under the quivering chin. She unlooped the halter from the high strength of the neck
And the arch the storm-cloud mane hung with live darkness. He stood; she crushed her breasts
On the hard shoulder, an arm over the withers, the other under the mass of his throat, and murmuring
Like a mountain dove, "If I could bear you." No way, no help, a gulf in nature. She murmured, "Come,
We will run on the hill. O beautiful, O beautiful," and led him to the gate and flung the bars on the ground. He threw his head downward
To snuff at the bars; and while he stood, she catching mane and withers with all sudden contracture
And strength of her lithe body, leaped, clung hard, and was mounted. He had been ridden before; he did not
Fight the weight but ran like a stone falling;
Broke down the slope into the moon-glass of the stream, and flattened to his neck
She felt the branches of a buck-eye tree fly over her, saw the wall of the oak-scrub
End her world: but he turned there, the matted branches
Scraped her right knee, the great slant shoulders

Laboring the hill-slope, up, up, the clear hill. Desire had
died in her
At the first rush, the falling like death, but now it
revived,
She feeling between her thighs the labor of the great
engine, the running muscles, the hard swiftness,
She riding the savage and exultant strength of the world.
Having topped the thicket he turned eastward,
Running less wildly; and now at length he felt the halter
when she drew on it; she guided him upward;
He stopped and grazed on the great arch and pride of
the hill, the silent calvary. A dwarfish oakwood
Climbed the other slope out of the dark of the unknown
canyon beyond; the last wind-beaten bush of it
Crawled up to the height, and California slipping from
her mount tethered him to it. She stood then,
Shaking. Enormous films of moonlight
Trailed down from the height. Space, anxious whiteness,
vastness. Distant beyond conception the shining
ocean
Lay light like a haze along the ledge and doubtful world's
end. Little vapors gleaming, and little
Darknesses on the far chart underfoot symbolized wood
and valley; but the air was the element, the moon-
Saturate arcs and spires of the air.
Here is solitude, here on the
calvary, nothing conscious
But the possible God and the cropped grass, no witness,

no eye but that misformed one, the moon's past fullness.

Two figures on the shining hill, woman and stallion, she kneeling to him, brokenly adoring.

He cropping the grass, shifting his hooves, or lifting the long head to gaze over the world,

Tranquil and powerful. She prayed aloud, "O God, I am not good enough, O fear, O strength, I am draggled.

Johnny and other men have had me, and O clean power! Here am I," she said, falling before him,

And crawled to his hooves. She lay a long while, as if asleep, in reach of the fore-hooves, weeping. He avoided

Her head and the prone body. He backed at first; but later plucked the grass that grew by her shoulder.

The small dark head under his nostrils: a small round stone, that smelt human, black hair growing from it:

The skull shut the light in it: it was not possible for any eyes

To know what throbbed and shone under the sutures of the skull, or a shell full of lightning

Had scared the roan strength, and he'd have broken tether, screaming, and run for the valley.

The atom bounds-breaking,

Nucleus to sun, electrons to planets, with recognition

Not praying, self-equaling, the whole to the whole, the microcosm
Not entering nor accepting entrance, more equally, more utterly, more incredibly conjugate
With the other extreme and greatness; passionately perceptive of identity. . . .
The fire threw up figures
And symbols meanwhile, racial myths formed and dissolved in it, the phantom rulers of humanity
That without being are yet more real than what they are born of, and without shape, shape that which makes them:
The nerves and the flesh go by shadowlike, the limbs and the lives shadowlike, these shadows remain, these shadows
To whom temples, to whom churches, to whom labors and wars, visions and dreams are dedicate:
Out of the fire in the small round stone that black moss covered, a crucified man writhed up in anguish;
A woman covered by a huge beast in whose mane the stars were netted, sun and moon were his eyeballs,
Smiled under the unendurable violation, her throat swollen with the storm and blood-flecks gleaming
On the stretched lips; a woman—no, a dark water, split by jets of lightning, and after a season
What floated up out of the furrowed water, a boat, a fish, a fire-globe?
It had wings, the creature,

And flew against the fountain of lightning, fell burnt out of the cloud back to the bottomless water . . .
Figures and symbols, castlings of the fire, played in her brain; but the white fire was the essence,
The burning in the small round shell of bone that black hair covered, that lay by the hooves on the hilltop.

She rose at length, she unknotted the halter; she walked and led the stallion; two figures, woman and stallion,
Came down the silent emptiness of the dome of the hill, under the cataract of the moonlight.

The next night there was moon through cloud. Johnny had returned half drunk toward evening, and California
Who had known him for years with neither love nor loathing to-night hating him had let the child Christine
Play in the light of the lamp for hours after her bedtime; who fell asleep at length on the floor
Beside the dog; then Johnny: "Put her to bed." She gathered the child against her breasts, she laid her
In the next room, and covered her with a blanket. The window was white, the moon had risen. The mother
Lay down by the child, but after a moment Johnny stood in the doorway. "Come drink." He had brought home

Two jugs of wine slung from the saddle, part payment for the stallion's service; a pitcher of it
Was on the table, and California sadly came and emptied her glass. Whisky, she thought,
Would have erased him till to-morrow; the thin red wine. . . . "We have a good evening," he laughed, pouring it.
"One glass yet then I show you what the red fellow did." She moving toward the house-door his eyes
Followed her, the glass filled and the red juice ran over the table. When it struck the floor-planks
He heard and looked. "Who stuck the pig?" he muttered stupidly, "here's blood, here's blood," and trailed his fingers
In the red lake under the lamplight. While he was looking down the door creaked, she had slipped out-doors,
And he, his mouth curving like a faun's, imagined the chase under the solemn redwoods, the panting
And unresistant victim caught in a dark corner. He emptied the glass and went out-doors
Into the dappled lanes of moonlight. No sound but the April brook's. "Hey Bruno," he called, "find her.
Bruno, go find her." The dog after a little understood and quested, the man following.
When California crouching by an oak-bush above the house heard them come near she darted
To the open slope and ran down hill. The dog barked at her heels, pleased with the game, and Johnny

Followed in silence. She ran down to the new corral, she saw the stallion
Move like a lion along the timbers of the fence, the dark arched neck shaking the nightfall
Of the great mane; she threw herself prone and writhed under the bars, his hooves backing away from her
Made muffled thunder in the soft soil. She stood in the midst of the corral, panting, but Johnny
Paused at the fence. The dog ran under it, and seeing the stallion move, the woman standing quiet,
Danced after the beast, with white-toothed feints and dashes. When Johnny saw the formidable dark strength
Recoil from the dog, he climbed up over the fence.

The child Christine waked when her mother left her
And lay half-dreaming, in the half-waking dream she saw the ocean come up out of the west
And cover the world, she looked up through clear water at the tops of the redwoods. She heard the door creak
And the house empty; her heart shook her body, sitting up on the bed, and she heard the dog
And crept toward light, where it gleamed under the crack of the door. She opened the door, the room was empty,
The table-top was a red lake under the lamplight. The color of it was terrible to her;

She had seen the red juice drip from a coyote's muzzle, her father had shot one day in the hills
And carried him home over the saddle: she looked at the rifle on the wall-rack: it was not moved:
She ran to the door, the dog was barking and the moon was shining: she knew wine by the odor
But the color frightened her, the empty house frightened her, she followed down hill in the white lane of moonlight
The friendly noise of the dog. She saw in the big horse's corral, on the level shoulder of the hill,
Black on white, the dark strength of the beast, the dancing fury of the dog, and the two others.
One fled, one followed; the big one charged, rearing; one fell under his fore-hooves. She heard her mother
Scream: without thought she ran to the house, she dragged a chair past the red pool and climbed to the rifle,
Got it down from the wall and lugged it somehow through the door and down the hillside, under the hard weight
Sobbing. Her mother stood by the rails of the corral, she gave it to her. On the far side
The dog flashed at the plunging stallion; in the midst of the space the man, slow-moving, like a hurt worm
Crawling, dragged his body by inches toward the fence-line. Then California, resting the rifle

On the top rail, without doubting, without hesitance,
Aimed for the leaping body of the dog, and when it
stood, fired. It snapped, rolled over, lay quiet.
"O mother, you've hit Bruno!" "I couldn't see the
sights in the moonlight," she answered quietly.
She stood
And watched, resting the rifle-butt on the ground. The
stallion wheeled, freed from his torment, the man
Lurched up to his knees, wailing a thin and bitter bird's
cry, and the roan thunder
Struck; hooves left nothing alive but teeth tore up the
remnant. "O mother, shoot, shoot!" Yet California
Stood carefully watching, till the beast having fed all
his fury stretched neck to utmost, head high,
And wrinkled back the upper lip from the teeth, yawn-
ing obscene disgust over—not a man—
A smear on the moon-lake earth: then California moved
by some obscure human fidelity
Lifted the rifle. Each separate nerve-cell of her brain
flaming the stars fell from their places
Crying in her mind: she fired three times before the
haunches crumpled sidewise, the forelegs stiffening,
And the beautiful strength settled to earth: she turned
then on her little daughter the mask of a woman
Who has killed God. The night-wind veering, the smell
of the spilt wine drifted down hill from the house.

I Hear an Army Charging upon the Land

JAMES JOYCE

I hear an army charging upon the land,
And the thunder of horses plunging, foam about their knees:
Arrogant, in black armour, behind them stand,
Disdaining the reins, with fluttering whips, the charioteers.

They cry unto the night their battle-name:
I moan in sleep when I hear afar their whirling laughter.
They cleave the gloom of dreams, a blinding flame,
Clanging, clanging upon the heart as upon an anvil.

They come shaking in triumph their long, green hair:
They come out of the sea and run shouting by the shore.
My heart, have you no wisdom thus to despair?
My love, my love, my love, why have you left me alone?

From *Not So Deep As a Well*

DOROTHY PARKER

1. Fighting Words

Say my love is easy had,
  Say I'm bitten raw with pride,
Say I am too often sad—
  Still behold me at your side.

Say I'm neither brave nor young,
  Say I woo and coddle care,
Say the devil touched my tongue—
  Still you have my heart to wear.

But say my verses do not scan,
  And I get me another man!

2. Bohemia

Authors and actors and artists and such
Never know nothing, and never know much.
Sculptors and singers and those of their kidney
Tell their affairs from Seattle to Sydney.
Playwrights and poets and such horses' necks
Start off from anywhere, end up at sex.
Diarists, critics and similar roe
Never say nothing, and never say no.
People who do things exceed my endurance;
God, for a man that solicits insurance!

The Monkeys

MARIANNE MOORE

winked too much and were afraid of snakes. The zebras,
supreme in
their abnormality; the elephants with their fog-coloured
skin
and strictly practical appendages
were there, the small cats; and the parrakeet—
trivial and humdrum on examination, destroying
bark and portions of the food it could not eat.

I recall their magnificence, now not more magnificent
than it is dim. It is difficult to recall the ornament,
speech, and precise manner of what one might
call the minor acquaintances twenty
years back; but I shall not forget him—that
Gilgamesh among
the hairy carnivora—that cat with the

wedge-shaped, slate-gray marks on its forelegs and the
resolute tail,
astringently remarking, 'They have imposed on us with
their pale
half-fledged protestations, trembling about
in inarticulate frenzy, saying
it is not for us to understand art; finding it
all so difficult, examining the thing

as if it were inconceivably arcanic, as symmet-
rically frigid as if it had been carved out of chrysophrase
or marble—strict with tension, malignant
in its power over us and deeper
than the sea when it proffers flattery in exchange
for hemp,
rye, flax, horses, platinum, timber, and fur.'

The Sea

D. H. LAWRENCE

You, you are all unloving, loveless, you;
Restless and lonely, shaken by your own moods,
You are celibate and single, scorning a comrade even,
Threshing your own passions with no woman for the threshing-floor,
Finishing your dreams for your own sake only,
Playing your great game around the world, alone,
Without playmate, or helpmate, having no one to cherish,
No one to comfort, and refusing any comforter.

Not like the earth, the spouse all full of increase
Moiled over with the rearing of her many-mouthed young;
You are single, you are fruitless, phosphorescent, cold and callous,
Naked of worship, of love or of adornment,
Scorning the panacea even of labour,
Sworn to a high and splendid purposelessness
Of brooding and delighting in the secret of life's goings,
Sea, only you are free, sophisticated.

You who toil not, you who spin not,
Surely but for you and your like, toiling
Were not worth while, nor spinning worth the effort!

You who take the moon as in a sieve, and sift
Her flake by flake and spread her meaning out;
You who roll the stars like jewels in your palm,
So that they seem to utter themselves aloud;
You who steep from out the days their colour,
Reveal the universal tint that dyes
Their web; who shadow the sun's great gestures and expressions
So that he seems a stranger in his passing;
Who voice the dumb night fittingly;
Sea, you shadow of all things, now mock us to death with your shadowing.

The Elephant Is Slow to Mate

D. H. LAWRENCE

The elephant, the huge old beast
  is slow to mate;
he finds a female, they show no haste
  they wait

for the sympathy in their vast shy hearts
  slowly, slowly to rouse
as they loiter along the river-beds
  and drink and browse

and dash in panic through the brake
  of forest with the herd,
and sleep in massive silence, and wake
  together, without a word.

So slowly the great hot elephant hearts
  grow full of desire,
and the great beasts mate in secret at last,
  hiding their fire.

Oldest they are and the wisest of beasts
  so they know at last
how to wait for the loneliest of feasts
  for the full repast.

They do not snatch, they do not tear;
their massive blood
moves as the moon-tides, near, more near
till they touch in flood.

From *The Ship of Death*

D. H. LAWRENCE

I sing of autumn and the falling fruit
and the long journey toward oblivion.

The apples falling like great drops of dew
to bruise themselves and exit from themselves.

Have you built your ship of death, oh, have you?

Build then your ship of death, for you will need it!

*

And if tonight my soul may find her peace
in sleep, and sink in good oblivion,
and in the morning wake like a new-opened flower
then I have been dipped again in God, and new-created.

And if, as weeks go round, in the dark of the moon
my spirit darkens and goes out, and soft strange gloom
pervades my movements and my thoughts and words
then I shall know that I am walking still
with God, we are close together now the moon's in
shadow.

And if, as autumn deepens and darkens
I feel the pain of falling leaves, and stems that break in
storms

and trouble and dissolution and distress
and then the softness of deep shadows folding, folding
around my soul and spirit, around my lips
so sweet, like a swoon, or more like the drowse of a low,
  sad song
singing darker than the nightingale, on, on to the solstice
and the silence of short days, the silence of the year, the
  shadow,
then I shall know that my life is moving still
with the dark earth, and drenched
with the deep oblivion of earth's lapse and renewal.

And if, in the changing phases of man's life
I fall in sickness and in misery
my wrists seem broken and my heart seems dead
and strength is gone, and my life
is only the leavings of a life:

and still, among it all, snatches of lovely oblivion, and
  snatches of renewal
odd, wintry flowers upon the withered stem, yet new,
  strange flowers
such as my life has not brought forth before, new blossoms of me—

then I must know that still
I am in the hands of the unknown God,
he is breaking me down to his own oblivion
to send me forth on a new morning, a new man.

Drift on, drift on, my soul, toward the most pure
most dark oblivion.
And at the penultimate porches, the dark-red mantle
of the body's memories slips and is absorbed
into the shell-like, womb-like convoluted shadow.

And round the great final bend of unbroken dark
the skirt of the spirit's experience has melted away
the oars have gone from the boat, and the little dishes
gone, gone, and the boat dissolves like pearl
as the soul at last slips perfect into the goal, the core
of sheer oblivion and of utter peace,
the womb of silence in the living night.

Ah peace, ah lovely peace, most lovely lapsing
of this my soul into the plasm of peace.

Oh lovely last, last lapse of death, into pure oblivion
at the end of the longest journey
peace, complete peace!
But can it be that also it is procreation?

*

Ah, if you want to live in peace on the face of the earth
Then build your ship of death, in readiness
For the longest journey, over the last of seas.

On the Vanity of Earthly Greatness

ARTHUR GUITERMAN

The tusks that clashed in mighty brawls
Of mastodons are billiard balls.

The sword of Charlemagne the Just
Is ferric oxide, known as rust.

The grizzly bear whose potent hug
Was feared by all is now a rug.

Great Caesar's bust is on the shelf,
And I don't feel so well myself!

Pied Beauty

GERARD MANLEY HOPKINS

Glory be to God for dappled things—
For skies of couple-colour as a brinded cow;
For rose-moles all in stipple upon trout that swim;
Fresh-firecoal chestnut-falls; finches' wings;
Landscape plotted and pieced—fold, fallow, and plough;
And áll trádes, their gear and tackle and trim.
All things counter, original, spare, strange;
Whatever is fickle, freckled (who knows how?)
With swift, slow; sweet, sour; adazzle, dim;
He fathers-forth whose beauty is past change:
Praise him.

Duns Scotus's Oxford

GERARD MANLEY HOPKINS

Towery city and branchy between towers;
Cuckoo-echoing, bell-swarméd, lark-charméd, rook-
racked, river-rounded;
The dapple-eared lily below thee; that country and
town did
Once encounter in, here coped and poiséd powers;

Thou hast a base and brickish skirt there, sours
That neighbour-nature thy grey beauty is grounded
Best in; graceless growth, thou hast confounded
Rural rural keeping—folk, flocks and flowers.

Yet ah! this air I gather and I release
He lived on; these weeds and waters, these walls are
what
He haunted who of all men most sways my spirits to
peace;
Of realty the rarest-veinéd unraveller; a not
Rivalled insight, be rival Italy or Greece;
Who fired France for Mary without spot.

Fragment

GERARD MANLEY HOPKINS

Strike, churl; hurl, cheerless wind, then; heltering hail
May's beauty massacre and wispéd wild clouds grow
Out on the giant air; tell Summer No,
Bid joy back, have at the harvest, keep Hope pale.

Felix Randal

GERARD MANLEY HOPKINS

Felix Randal the farrier, O he is dead then? my duty all
ended,
Who have watched his mould of man, big-boned and
hardy-handsome
Pining, pining, till time when reason rambled in it and
some
Fatal four disorders, fleshed there, all contended?

Sickness broke him. Impatient he cursed at first, but
mended
Being anointed and all; though a heavenlier heart
began some
Months earlier, since I had our sweet reprieve and
ransom
Tendered to him. Ah well, God rest him all road ever
he offended!

This seeing the sick endears them to us, us too it endears.
My tongue had taught thee comfort, touch had quenched
thy tears,
Thy tears that touched my heart, child, Felix, poor Felix
Randal;

How far from then forethought of, all thy more boister-
ous years,

When thou at the random grim forge, powerful amidst peers,
Didst fettle for the great grey drayhorse his bright and battering sandal!

Little Ivory Figures Pulled with String

AMY LOWELL

Is it the tinkling of mandolins which disturbs you?
Or the dropping of bitter-orange petals among the coffee-
    cups?
Or the slow creeping of the moonlight between the olive-
    trees?
  Drop! drop! the rain
  Upon the thin plates of my heart.

String your blood to chord with this music,
Stir your heels upon the cobbles to the rhythm of a
    dance-tune.
They have slim thighs and arms of silver;
The moon washes away their garments;
They make a pattern of fleeing feet in the branch
    shadows,
And the green grapes knotted about them
Burst as they press against one another.
  The rain knocks upon the plates of my heart,
  They are crumpled with its beating.

Would you drink only from your brains, Old Man?
See, the moonlight has reached your knees,
It falls upon your head in an accolade of silver.
Rise up on the music,

Fling against the moon-drifts in a whorl of young light
bodies:
Leaping grape-clusters,
Vine leaves tearing from a grey wall.
You shall run, laughing, in a braid of women,
And weave flowers with the frosty spines of thorns.
Why do you gaze into your glass,
And jar the spoons with your finger-tapping?
The rain is rigid on the plates of my heart.
The murmur of it is loud—loud.

I Am of Ireland

W. B. YEATS

"I am of Ireland,
And the Holy Land of Ireland,
And time runs on," cried she.
"Come out of charity,
Come dance with me in Ireland."

One man, one man alone
In that outlandish gear,
One solitary man
Of all that rambled there
Had turned his stately head.
"That is a long way off,
And time runs on," he said,
"And the night grows rough."

"I am of Ireland,
And the Holy Land of Ireland,
And time runs on," cried she,
"Come out of charity
And dance with me in Ireland."

"The fiddlers are all thumbs,
Or the fiddle-strings accursed,
The drums and the kettle-drums
And the trumpets all are burst,

And the trombone," cried he,
"The trumpet and trombone,"
And cocked a malicious eye,
"But time runs on, runs on."

"I am of Ireland,
And the Holy Land of Ireland,
And time runs on," cried she.
"Come out of charity
And dance with me in Ireland."

Swift's Epitaph

W. B. YEATS

Swift has sailed into his rest;
Savage indignation there
Cannot lacerate his breast.
Imitate him if you dare,
World-besotted traveler; he
Served human liberty.

The Dedication to a Book of Stories Selected from the Irish Novelists

W. B. YEATS

There was a green branch hung with many a bell
When her own people ruled this tragic Eire;
And from its murmuring greenness, calm of Faery,
A Druid kindness, on all hearers fell.

It charmed away the merchant from his guile
And turned the farmer's memory from his cattle,
And hushed in sleep the roaring ranks of battle:
And all grew friendly for a little while.

Ah, Exiles wandering over lands and seas,
And planning, plotting always that some morrow
May set a stone upon ancestral Sorrow!
I also bear a bell-branch full of ease.

I tore it from green boughs winds tore and tossed
Until the sap of summer had grown weary!
I tore it from the barren boughs of Eire,
That country where a man can be so crossed;

Can be so battered, badgered and destroyed
That he's a loveless man: gay bells bring laughter
That shakes a mouldering cobweb from the rafter;
And yet the saddest chimes are best enjoyed.

Gay bells or sad, they bring you memories
Of half-forgotten innocent old places:
We and our bitterness have left no traces
On Munster grass and Connemara skies.

The Cold Heaven

W. B. YEATS

Suddenly I saw the cold and rook-delighting Heaven
That seemed as though ice burned and was but the more
  ice,
And thereupon imagination and heart were driven
So wild that every casual thought of that and this
Vanished, and left but memories, that should be out of
  season
With the hot blood of youth, of love crossed long ago;
And I took all the blame out of all sense and reason,
Until I cried and trembled and rocked to and fro,
Riddled with light. Ah! when the ghost begins to
  quicken,
Confusion of the death-bed over, is it sent
Out naked on the roads, as the books say, and stricken
By the injustice of the skies for punishment?

Sailing to Byzantium

W. B. YEATS

1.

That is no country for old men. The young
In one another's arms; birds in the trees,
—Those dying generations—at their song;
The salmon-falls, the mackerel-crowded seas,
Fish, flesh, or fowl, commend all summer long
Whatever is begotten, born, and dies.
Caught in that sensual music all neglect
Monuments of unageing intellect.

2.

An aged man is but a paltry thing,
A tattered coat upon a stick, unless
Soul clap its hands and sing, and louder sing
For every tatter in its mortal dress,
Nor is there singing school but studying
Monuments of its own magnificence;
And therefore I have sailed the seas and come
To the holy city of Byzantium.

3.

O sages standing in God's holy fire
As in the gold mosaic of a wall,
Come from the holy fire, perne in a gyre,
And be the singing masters of my soul.

Consume my heart away; sick with desire
And fastened to a dying animal
It knows not what it is; and gather me
Into the artifice of eternity.

4.

Once out of nature I shall never take
My bodily form from any natural thing,
But such a form as Grecian goldsmiths make
Of hammered gold and gold enamelling
To keep a drowsy emperor awake;
Or set upon a golden bough to sing
To lords and ladies of Byzantium
Of what is past, or passing, or to come.

PART TWO

Who can make a poem of the depths of weariness
bringing meaning to those never in the depths?
Those who order what they please
when they choose to have it—
can they understand the many down under
who come home to their wives and children at night
and night after night as yet too brave and unbroken
to say, "I ache all over"?
How can a poem deal with production cost
and leave out definite misery paying
a permanent price in shattered health and early old age?
When will the efficiency engineers and the poets
get together on a program?
Will that be a cold day? will that be a special hour?
Will somebody be coocoo then?
And if so, who?
And what does the Christian Bible say?
And the Mohammedan Koran and Confucius and the Shintoists
and the Encyclicals of the Popes?
Will somebody be coocoo then?
And if so, who??

—Carl Sandburg

A Group of Negro Songs

ANONYMOUS

1.

I know moon-rise, I know star-rise,
  I lay dis body down.
I walk in de moonlight, I walk in de starlight
  To lay dis body down.
I walk in de graveyard, I walk through the graveyard
  To lay dis body down.
I lie in de grave an' stretch out my arms;
  Lay dis body down.
I go to de judgement in de evenin' of de day
  When I lay dis body down
An' my soul and your soul will meet in de day
  When I lay dis body down.

2.

Joshua fit de battle ob Jerico,
  Jerico, Jerico,—
Joshua fit de battle ob Jerico
  An de walls come tumblin' down.

You may talk about yo' king ob Gideon,
You may talk about yo' man ob Saul;
Dere's none like good ole Josh-ua
At de battle ob Jerico.

Up to de walls ob Jerico
He marched with spear in han';
"Go blow dem ram horns," Joshua cried,
"Kase de battle am in my han'."

Den de lam' ram sheep horns begin to blow,
Trumpets begin to soun';
Josh-u-a commanded de chillun to shout
An' de walls come tumblin' down;

Dat mornin'
Joshua fit de battle ob Jerico,
Jerico, Jerico;
Joshua fit de battle ob Jerico
An' de walls come tumblin' down.

3.

Dark was de night an' col' was de groun'
In which de Lawd was laid,
Sweat like blood run down in drops
An' in agony he prayed.

4.

Yes, the book of Revelations will be brought forth dat day,
An' every leaf unfolded, the book of the seven seals.

An' I went down to Egypt, I camped upon de groun'
At de soundin' of de trumpet de Holy Ghost came down.

And when de seals were opened, the voice said, "Come an' see,"
I went an' stood a-looking to see de mystery.

The red horse came a-gallopin', and de black horse he came too,
An' de pale horse he came down de road, an' stole my father away.

An' den I see ole Satan, an' dey bound him wid a chain,
An' dey put him in de fi-ar an' I see de smoke arise.

Dey bound him in de fi-ar, where he wanted to take my soul,
Ole Satan gnashed his teeth and howled, he missed po' sinner man's soul.

Den I see de dead arisin', and stan' before de Lamb
And de wicked call on de mountains to hide dem f'om His face,

An' den I see de Christians, standin' on God's right hand
A-shoutin' "Hallelujah!" singing praises to de Lord.

5.

When de golden trumpets sound
Where will yo' soul be found?
Standin' aroun', standin' around
When de golden trumpets sound.

When de golden trumpets sound
Where will my soul be found?
With de crowned, with de crowned
When de golden trumpets sound.

6.

I wrastled wid Satan, I wrastled wid sin,
Stepped over hell, an' come back ag'in.

Isaiah mounted on de wheel of time,
Spoke to God A-mighty way down de line.

O hear dat lumberin' thunder
A-roll f'om door to door,
A-callin' de people home to God,
Dey'll git home bime-by.

O see dat forkéd lightnin'
A-jump f'om cloud to cloud,
A-pickin' up God's chillun,
Dey'll git home bime-by.

7.

Sometimes I feel like an eagle in de air
Some-a dese mornin's bright an' fair
I'm goin' to lay down my heavy load;
Goin' to spread my wings an' cleave de air.
You may bury me in de east,
You may bury me in de west,

But I'll hear de trumpet sound
In-a dat mornin'.

8.

John Henry tol' his Cap'n
That a man was a natch'al man:
And before he'd let that steam drill beat him down
He'd fall dead wid his hammer in his han'
He'd fall dead wid his hammer in his han'.

John Henry says to his Cap'n
"Send me a twelve-poun' hammer aroun',
A twelve-poun' wid a four-foot handle
And I beat yo' steam drill down,
And I beat yo' steam drill down."

John Henry says to his shaker
"Look hear, man, why don't you sing?
I'm throwin' twelve-poun' from my hips on down,
Jes' you listen to do col' steel ring,
Jes' you lis'en to de col' steel ring."

John Henry went down on de railroad
Wid a twelve-poun' hammer by his side,
He walked down de track but he never come back,
'Cause he laid down his hammer an' he died,
'Cause he laid down his hammer an' he died.

John Henry had a good woman,
Her name was Polly Ann.

On de day John Henry he dropped dead
Polly Ann hammered steel like a man.
Polly Ann hammered steel like a man.

TWO SONGS BY W. C. HANDY

Fragment from "Sundown Blues"

Copyright 1923 by W. C. Handy.

Published by Handy Bros. Music Co., Inc., New York.
Reprinted by permission.

I've put some
Ashes in my sweet papa's bed,
So that he can't slip out —
Hoodoo in his bread,
Goopher-dust all about — *I'll fix him!*
Con - ju - ra - tion
Is in his socks and shoes;
Tomorrow he will have those
Mean Sundown Blues!

St. Louis Blues

Copyright 1914 by W. C. Handy.

Published by Handy Bros. Music Co., Inc., New York.
Reprinted by permission.

Ah hate to see de evenin' sun go down,
Hate to see de evenin' sun go down —

'Cause my baby — he done lef' dis town
Feelin' tomorrow lak Ah feel today,
Feel tomorrow lak Ah feel today,
Ah'll pack mah trunk, make mah getaway.
St. Louis 'oman wid her di'mon' rings
Pulls dat man 'roun' by her apron strings;
'Twant for powder an' for store-bought hair
De man Ah love would not gone nowhere.

You ought to see dat stove-pipe brown of mine
Lak he own de Di'mon' Joseph Line;
He'd make a cross-eyed 'oman go stone blin'.
Blacker than midnight, teeth lak flags of truce,
Blackest man in de whole St. Louis,
Blacker de berry — sweeter is de juice.
About a crap game he knows a pow'ful lot
But when work-time comes he's on de dot;
Gwine to ask him for a cold ten spot:
What it takes to git it, he's cert'nly got.

Got de St. Louis Blues, jes' blue as Ah can be
Dat man got a heart lak a rock cast in de sea
Or else he wouldn't gone so far from me.

The Man with the Hoe

EDWIN MARKHAM

God made man in his own image
in the image of God he made him.—Genesis.

Bowed by the weight of centuries he leans
Upon his hoe and gazes on the ground,
The emptiness of ages in his face,
And on his back the burden of the world.
Who made him dead to rapture and despair,
A thing that grieves not and that never hopes,
Stolid and stunned, a brother to the ox?
Who loosened and let down this brutal jaw?
Whose was the hand that slanted back this brow?
Whose breath blew out the light within this brain?

Is this the Thing the Lord God made and gave
To have dominion over sea and land?
To trace the stars and search the heavens for power;
To feel the passion of Eternity?
Is this the dream He dreamed who shaped the suns
And markt their ways upon the ancient deep?
Down all the caverns of Hell to their last gulf
There is no shape more terrible than this—
More tongued with censure of the world's blind greed—
More filled with signs and portents for the soul—
More packt with danger to the universe.

What gulfs between him and the seraphim!
Slave of the wheel of labor, what to him
Are Plato and the swing of Pleiades?
What the long reaches of the peaks of song,
The rift of dawn, the reddening of the rose?
Through this dread shape the suffering ages look;
Time's tragedy is in that aching stoop;
Through this dread shape humanity betrayed,
Plundered, profaned and disinherited,
Cries protest to the Powers that made the world,
A protest that is also prophecy.

O masters, lords and rulers in all lands,
Is this the handiwork you give to God,
This monstrous thing distorted and soul-quencht?
How will you ever straighten up this shape;
Touch it again with immortality;
Give back the upward looking and the light;
Rebuild in it the music and the dream;
Make right the immemorial infamies,
Perfidious wrongs, immedicable woes?

O masters, lords and rulers in all lands,
How will the future reckon with this Man?
How answer his brute question in that hour
When whirlwinds of rebellion shake all shores?
How will it be with kingdoms and with kings—
With those who shaped him to the thing he is—
When this dumb Terror shall rise to judge the world,
After the silence of the centuries?

Through the Needle's Eye

SARAH N. CLEGHORN

1. Comrade Jesus

Thanks to Saint Matthew, who had been
At mass meetings in Palestine,
We know whose side was spoken for
When Comrade Jesus had the floor.

"Where sore they toil and hard they lie,
Among the great unwashed, dwell I.
The tramp, the convict, I am he;
Cold-shoulder him, cold-shoulder me."

By Dives' door, with thoughtful eye,
He did tomorrow prophesy.
"The kingdom's gate is low and small;
The rich can scarce wedge through at all."

"A dangerous man," said Caiaphas,
"An ignorant demagogue, alas,
Friend of low women, it is he
Slanders the upright Pharisee."

For law and order, it was plain
For holy church, he must be slain.
The troops were there to awe the crowd
And "violence" was not allowed.

Their clumsy force with force to foil
His strong, clean hands he would not soil.
He saw their childishness quite plain
Between the lightnings of his pain.

Between the twilights of his end
He made his fellow-felon friend;
With swollen tongue and blinding eyes
Invited him to paradise.

2. Quatrain

The golf links lie so near the mill
  That almost every day
The laboring children can look out
  And see the men at play.

From *Spoon River*

EDGAR LEE MASTERS

1. Mrs. Williams

I was the milliner
Talked about, lied about,
Mother of Dora,
Whose strange disappearance
Was charged to her rearing.
My eye quick to beauty
Saw much beside ribbons
And buckles and feathers
And leghorns and felts,
To set off sweet faces,
And dark hair and gold.
One thing I will tell you
And one I will ask:
The stealers of husbands
Wear powder and trinkets,
And fashionable hats.
Wives, wear them yourselves.
Hats may make divorces—
They also prevent them.
Well now, let me ask you:
If all of the children, born here in Spoon River
Had been reared by the County, somewhere on a farm;
And the fathers and mothers had been given their free-
dom

To live and enjoy, change mates if they wished,
Do you think that Spoon River
Had been any the worse?

2. Chandler Nicholas

Every morning bathing myself and shaving myself,
And dressing myself.
But no one in my life to take delight
In my fastidious appearance.
Every day walking, and deep breathing
For the sake of my health.
But to what use vitality?
Every day improving my mind
With meditation and reading,
But no one with whom to exchange wisdoms.
No agora, no clearing house
For ideas, Spoon River.
Seeking, but never sought;
Ripe, companionable, useful, but useless.
Chained here in Spoon River,
My liver scorned by the vultures,
And self-devoured!

3. Howard Lamson

Ice cannot shiver in the cold,
Nor stones shrink from the lapping flame.
Eyes that are sealed no more have tears;
Ears that are stopped hear nothing ill;

Hearts turned to silt are strange to pain;
Tongues that are dumb report no loss;
Hands stiffened, well may idle be;
No sigh is from a breathless breast.
Beauty may fade, but closed eyes see not;
Sorrow may wail, but stopped ears hear not;
Nothing to say is for dumb tongues.
The rolling earth rolls on and on
With trees and stones and winding streams—
My dream is what the hillside dreams!

Miniver Cheevy

EDWIN ARLINGTON ROBINSON

Miniver Cheevy, child of scorn
  Grew lean while he assailed the seasons;
He wept that he was ever born,
  And he had reasons.

Miniver loved the days of old
  When swords were bright and steeds were prancing;
The vision of a warrior bold
  Would set him dancing.

Miniver sighed for what was not,
  And dreamed, and rested from his labors;
He dreamed of Thebes and Camelot,
  And Priam's neighbors.

Miniver mourned the ripe renown
  That made so many a name so fragrant;
He mourned Romance, now on the town,
  And Art, a vagrant.

Miniver loved the Medici,
  Albeit he had never seen one;
He would have sinned incessantly
  Could he have been one.

Miniver cursed the commonplace
  And eyed a khaki suit with loathing;
He missed the medieval grace
  Of iron clothing.

Miniver scorned the gold he sought,
  But sore annoyed was he without it;
Miniver thought, and thought, and thought
  And thought about it.

Miniver Cheevy, born too late,
  Scratched his head and kept on thinking;
Miniver coughed, and called it fate,
  And kept on drinking.

The Man Against the Sky

EDWIN ARLINGTON ROBINSON

Between me and the sunset, like a dome
Against the glory of a world on fire,
Now burned a sudden hill,
Bleak, round and high, by flame-lit height made higher,
With nothing on it for the flame to kill
Save one who moved and was alone up there
To loom before the chaos and the glare
As if he were the last god going home
Unto his last desire.
Dark, marvellous, and inscrutable he moved on
Till down the fiery distance he was gone,
Like one of those eternal, remote things
That range across a man's imaginings
When a sure music fills him and he knows
What he may say thereafter to few men—
The touch of ages having wrought
An echo and a glimpse of what he thought
A phantom or a legend until then;
For whether lighted over ways that save,
Or lured from all repose,
If he go on too far to find a grave,
Mostly alone he goes.

Even he, who stood where I had found him,
On high with fire all round him,

Who moved along the molten west,
And over the round hill's crest
That seemed half ready with him to go down,
Flame-bitten and flame-cleft
As if there were to be no last thing left
Of a nameless unimaginable town–
Even he who climbed and vanished may have taken
Down to the perils of a depth not known,
From death defended, though by men forsaken,
The bread that every man must eat alone;
He may have walked while others hardly dared
Look on to see him stand where many fell;
And upward out of that as out of hell,
He may have sung and striven
To mount where more of him shall yet be given,
Bereft of all retreat,
To sevenfold heat–
As on a day when three in Dura shared
The furnace, and were spared
For glory by that king of Babylon
Who made himself so great that God, who heard,
Covered him with long feathers, like a bird.

Again, he may have gone down easily,
By comfortable altitudes, and found,
As always, underneath him solid ground
Whereon to be sufficient and to stand
Possessed already of the promised land,
Far stretched and fair to see:

A good sight, verily,
And one to make the eyes of her who bore him
Shine glad with hidden tears.
Why question of his ease of who before him,
In one place or another where they left
Their names as far behind them as their bones
And yet by dint of slaughter, toil, and theft,
And shrewdly sharpened stones,
Carved hard the way for his ascendancy
Through deserts of lost years?
Why trouble him now who sees and hears
No more than what his innocence requires,
And therefore to no other height aspires
Than one at which he neither quails nor tires?
He may do more by seeing what he sees
Than others eager for iniquities;
He may, by seeing all things for the best,
Incite futurity to do the rest.

Or with an even likelihood,
He may have met with atrabilious eyes
The fires of time on equal terms and passed
Indifferently down, until at last
His only kind of grandeur would have been,
Apparently, in being seen.
He may have had for evil or for good
No argument; he may have had no care
For what without himself went anywhere
To failure or to glory, and least of all

For such a stale, flamboyant miracle;
He may have been the prophet of an art
Immovable to old idolatries;
He may have been a player without a part,
Annoyed that even the sun should have the skies
For such a flaming way to advertise;
He may have been a painter sick at heart
With Nature's toiling for a new surprise;
He may have been a cynic, who now, for all
Of anything divine that his effete
Negation may have tasted,
Saw truth in his own image, rather small,
Forbore to fever the ephemeral,
Found any barren height a good retreat
From any swarming street,
And in the sun saw power superbly wasted;
And when the primitive old-fashioned stars
Came out again to shine on joys and wars
More primitive, and all arrayed for doom,
He may have proved a world a sorry thing
In his imagining,
And life a lighted highway to the tomb.

Or, mounting with unfirm unsearching tread,
His hopes to chaos led,
He may have stumbled up there from the past,
And with an aching strangeness viewed the last
Abysmal conflagration of his dreams—
A flame where nothing seems

To burn but flame itself, by nothing fed;
And while it all went out,
Not even the faint anodyne of doubt
May then have eased a painful going down
From pictured heights of power and lost renown,
Revealed at length to his outlived endeavour
Remote and unapproachable forever;
And at his heart there may have gnawed
Sick memories of a dead faith foiled and flawed
And long dishonoured by the living death
Assigned alike by chance
To brutes and hierophants;
And anguish fallen on those he loved around him
May once have dealt the last blow to confound him,
And so have left him as death leaves a child,
Who sees it all too near;
And he who knows no young way to forget
May struggle to the tomb unreconciled.
Whatever suns may rise or set
There may be nothing kinder for him here
Than shafts and agonies;
And under these
He may cry out and stay on horribly;
Or, seeing in death too small a thing to fear,
He may go forward like a stoic Roman
Where pangs and terrors in his pathway lie—
Or, seizing the swift logic of a woman,
Curse God and die.

Or maybe there, like many another one
Who might have stood aloft and looked ahead,
Black-drawn against wild red,
He may have built unawed by fiery gules
That in him no commotion stirred,
A living reason out of molecules
Why molecules occurred,
And one for smiling when he might have sighed
Had he seen far enough
And in the same inevitable stuff
Discovered an odd reason too for pride
In being what he must have been by laws
Infrangible and for no kind of cause.
Deterred by no confusion or surprise
He may have seen with his mechanic eyes
A world without a meaning, and had room,
Alone amid magnificence and doom,
To build himself an airy monument
That should, or fail him in his vague intent,
Outlast an accidental universe–
To call it nothing worse–
Or, by the burrowing guile
Of Time disintegrated and effaced,
Like once-remembered mighty trees go down
To ruin, of which by man may now be traced
No part sufficient even to be rotten,
And in the book of things that are forgotten
Is entered as a thing not quite worth while.
He may have been so great

That satraps would have shivered at his frown,
And all he prized alive may rule a state
No larger than a grave that holds a clown;
He may have been a master of his fate,
And of his atoms—ready as another
In his emergence to exonerate
His father and his mother;
He may have been a captain of a host,
Self-eloquent and ripe for prodigies,
Doomed here to swell by dangerous degrees,
And then give up the ghost.
Nahum's great grasshoppers were such as these,
Sun-scattered and soon lost.

Whatever the dark road he may have taken,
This man who stood on high
And faced alone the sky,
Whatever drove or lured or guided him—
A vision answering a faith unshaken,
An easy trust assumed of easy trials,
A sick negation born of weak denials,
A crazed abhorrence of an old condition,
A blind attendance on a brief ambition—
Whatever stayed him or derided him,
His way was even as ours;
And we, with all our wounds and all our powers,
Must each await alone at his own height
Another darkness or another light;

And there, of our poor self dominion reft,
If inference and reason shun
Hell, Heaven, and Oblivion,
May thwarted will (perforce precarious,
But for our conservation better thus)
Have no misgiving left
Of doing yet what here we leave undone?
Or if unto the last of these we cleave,
Believing or protesting we believe
In such an idle and ephemeral
Florescence of the diabolical—
If, robbed of two fond old enormities,
Our being had no onward auguries,
What then were this great love of ours to say
For launching other lives to voyage again
A little farther into time and pain,
A little faster in a futile chase
For a kingdom and a power and a Race
That would have still in sight
A manifest end of ashes and eternal night?
Is this the music of the toys we shake
So loud—as if there might be no mistake
Somewhere in our indomitable will?
Are we no greater than the noise we make
Along our blind atomic pilgrimage
Whereon by crass chance billeted we go
Because our brains and bones and cartilage
Will have it so?

If this we say, then let us all be still
About our share in it, and live and die
More quietly thereby.

Where was he going, this man against the sky?
You know not, nor do I.
But this we know, if we know anything:
That we may laugh and fight and sing
And of our transcience here make offering
To an orient Word that will not be erased,
Or, save in incommunicable gleams
Too permanent for dreams,
Be found or known.
No tonic or ambitious irritant
Of increase or of want
Has made an otherwise insensate waste
Of ages overthrown
A ruthless, veiled, implacable foretaste
Of other ages that are still to be
Depleted and rewarded variously
Because a few, by fate's economy
Shall seem to move the world the way it goes,
No soft evangel of equality,
Safe-cradled in a communal repose
That huddles into death and may at last
Be covered well with equatorial snows—
And all for what, the devil only knows—
Will aggregate an inkling to confirm
The credit of a sage or of a worm,

Or tell us why one man in five
Should have a care to stay alive
While in his heart he feels no violence
Laid on his humour and intelligence
When infant Science makes a pleasant face
And waves again that hollow toy, the Race;
No planetary trap where souls are wrought
For nothing but the sake of being caught
And sent again to nothing will attune
Itself to any key of any reason
Why man should hunger through another season
To find out why 'twere better late than soon
To go away and let the sun and moon
And all the silly stars illuminate
A place for creeping things,
And those that root and trumpet and have wings,
And herd and ruminate,
Or dive and flash and poise in rivers and seas,
Or by their loyal tails in lofty trees
Hang screeching lewd victorious derision
Of man's immortal vision.

Shall we, because Eternity records
Too vast an answer for the time-born words
We spell, whereof so many are dead that once
In our capricious lexicons
Were so alive and final, hear no more
The Word itself, the living word
That none alive has ever heard

Or ever spelt,
And few have ever felt
Without the fears and old surrenderings
And terrors that began
When Death let fall a feather from his wings
And humbled the first man?
Because the weight of our humility,
Wherefrom we gain
A little wisdom and much pain,
Falls here too sore and there too tedious,
Are we in anguish or complacency,
Not looking far enough ahead
To see by what mad couriers we are led
Along the roads of the ridiculous,
To pity ourselves and laugh at faith
And while we curse life bear it?
And if we see the soul's dead end in death,
Are we to fear it?
What folly is here that has not yet a name
Unless we say outright that we are liars?
What have we seen beyond our sunset fires
That lights again the way by which we came?
Why pay we such a price, and one we give
So clamouringly, for each racked empty day
That leads one more last human hope away,
As quiet fiends would lead past our crazed eyes
Our children to an unseen sacrifice?
If after all that we have lived and thought,
All comes to Nought—

If there be nothing after Now,
And we be nothing anyhow,
And we know that—why live?
'Twere sure but weaklings' vain distress
To suffer dungeons where so many doors
Will open on the cold eternal shores
That look sheer down
To the dark tideless floods of Nothingness
Where all who know may drown.

George Crabbe

EDWIN ARLINGTON ROBINSON

Give him the darkest inch your shelf allows,
Hide him in lonely garrets, if you will,—
But his hard, human pulse is throbbing still
With the sure strength that fearless truth endows.
In spite of all fine science disavows,
Of his plain excellence and stubborn skill
There yet remains what fashion cannot kill,
Though years have thinned the laurel from his brows.

Whether or not we read him, we can feel
From time to time the vigor of his name
Against us like a finger for the shame
And emptiness of what our souls reveal
In books that are as altars where we kneel
To consecrate the flicker, not the flame.

Two Tramps in Mud Time

ROBERT FROST

Out of the mud two strangers came
And caught me splitting wood in the yard.
And one of them put me off my aim
By hailing cheerily "Hit them hard!"
I knew pretty well why he dropped behind
And let the other go on a way.
I knew pretty well what he had in mind:
He wanted to take my job for pay.

Good blocks of beech it was I split,
As large around as the chopping block;
And every piece I squarely hit
Fell splinterless as a cloven rock.
The blows that a life of self-control
Spares to strike for the common good
That day, giving a loose to my soul,
I spent on the unimportant wood.

The sun was warm but the wind was chill.
You know how it is with an April day
When the sun is out and the wind is still,
You're one month on in the middle of May.
But if you so much as dare to speak,
A cloud comes over the sunlit arch,
A wind comes off a frozen peak,
And you're two months back in the middle of March.

A bluebird comes tenderly up to alight
And fronts the wind to unruffle a plume,
His song so pitched as not to excite
A single flower as yet to bloom.
It is snowing a flake: and he half knew
Winter was only playing possum.
Except in color he isn't blue,
But he wouldn't advise a thing to blossom.

The water for which we may have to look
In summertime with a witching-wand,
In every wheelrut's now a brook,
In every print of a hoof a pond.
Be glad of water, but don't forget
The lurking frost in the earth beneath
That will steal forth after the sun is set
And show on the water its crystal teeth.

The time when most I loved my task
These two must make me love it more
By coming with what they came to ask.
You'd think I never had felt before
The weight of an ax-head poised aloft,
The grip on earth of outspread feet,
The life of muscles rocking soft
And smooth and moist in vernal heat.

Out of the woods two hulking tramps
(From sleeping God knows where last night,

But not long since in the lumber camps).
They thought all chopping was theirs of right.
Men of the woods and lumberjacks,
They judged me by their appropriate tool.
Except as a fellow handled an ax,
They had no way of knowing a fool.

Nothing on either side was said.
They knew they had but to stay their stay
And all their logic would fill my head:
As that I had no right to play
With what was another man's work for gain.
My right might be love but theirs was need.
And where the two exist in twain
Theirs was the better right—agreed.

But yield who will to their separation,
My object in living is to unite
My avocation and my vocation
As my two eyes make one in sight.
Only where love and need are one,
And the work is play for mortal stakes,
Is the deed ever really done
For Heaven and the future's sakes.

The Fear

ROBERT FROST

A lantern light from deeper in the barn
Shone on a man and woman in the door
And threw their lurching shadows on a house
Near by, all dark in every glossy window.
A horse's hoof pawed once the hollow floor,
And the back of the gig they stood beside
Moved in a little. The man grasped a wheel,
The woman spoke out sharply, "Whoa, stand still!"
"I saw it just as plain as a white plate,"
She said, "as the light on the dashboard ran
Along the bushes at the roadside—a man's face.
You *must* have seen it too."

"I didn't see it.
Are you sure——"
"Yes, I'm sure!"
"——it was a face?"

"Joel, I'll have to look. I can't go in,
I can't, and leave a thing like that unsettled.
Doors locked and curtains drawn will make no difference.
I always have felt strange when we came home
To the dark house after so long an absence,
And the key rattled loudly into place

Seemed to warn someone to be getting out
At one door as we entered at another.
What if I'm right, and someone all the time—
Don't hold my arm!"

"I say it's someone passing."

"You speak as if this were a travelled road.
You forget where we are. What is beyond
That he'd be going to or coming from
At such an hour of night, and on foot too.
What was he standing still for in the bushes?"

"It's not so very late—it's only dark.
There's more in it than you're inclined to say.
Did he look like——?"

"He looked like anyone.
I'll never rest to-night unless I know.
Give me the lantern."

"You don't want the lantern."

She pushed past him and got it for herself.

"You're not to come," she said. "This is my business.
If the time's come to face it, I'm the one
To put it the right way. He'd never dare—
Listen! He kicked a stone. Hear that, hear that!

He's coming towards us. Joel, *go* in—please.
Hark!—I don't hear him now. But please go in."

"In the first place you can't make me believe it's——"

"It is—or someone else he's sent to watch.
And now's the time to have it out with him
While we know definitely where he is.
Let him get off and he'll be everywhere
Around us, looking out of trees and bushes
Till I shan't dare to set a foot outdoors.
And I can't stand it. Joe, let me go!"

"But it's nonsense to think he'd care enough."

"You mean you couldn't understand his caring.
Oh, but you see he hadn't had enough—
Joel, I won't—I won't—I promise you.
We mustn't say hard things. You mustn't either."

"I'll be the one, if anybody goes!
But you give him the advantage with this light
What couldn't he do to us standing here!
And if to see was what he wanted, why
He has seen all there was to see and gone."

He appeared to forget to keep his hold,
But advanced with her as she crossed the grass
"What do you want?" she cried to all the dark.

She stretched up tall to overlook the light
That hung in both hands hot against her skirt

"There's no one; so you're wrong," he said.

"There is—
What do you want?" she cried, and then herself
Was startled when an answer really came.

"Nothing." It came from well along the road.
She reached a hand to Joel for support:
The smell of scorching woolen made her faint.
"What are you doing round this house at night?"

"Nothing." A pause: there seemed no more to say.
And then the voice again: "You seem afraid,
I saw by the way you whipped up the horse.
I'll just come forward in the lantern light
And let you see."

"Yes, do—Joel, go back."
She stood her ground against the noisy steps
That came on, but her body rocked a little.

"You see," the voice said.

"Oh." She looked and looked.
"You don't see—I've a child here by the hand."

"What's a child doing at this time of night—?"

"Out walking. Every child should have the memory
Of at least one long-after-bedtime walk.
What, son?"

            "Then I should think you'd try to find
Somewhere to walk——"
                    "The highway as it happens—
We're stopping for the fortnight down at Dean's."
"But if that's all—Joel—you realize—
You won't think anything. You understand?
You understand that we have to be careful.
This is a very, very lonely place.
Joel!" She spoke as if she couldn't turn.
The swinging lantern lengthened to the ground,
It touched, it struck, it clattered and went out.

Abraham Lincoln Walks at Midnight

VACHEL LINDSAY

(In Springfield, Illinois)

It is portentous, and a thing of state
That here at midnight, in our little town
A mourning figure walks, and will not rest,
Near the old court-house pacing up and down,

Or by his homestead, or in shadowed yards
He lingers where his children used to play,
Or through the market, on the well-worn stones
He stalks until the dawn-stars burn away.

A bronzed, lank man! His suit of ancient black,
A famous high top-hat and plain worn shawl
Make him the quaint great figure that men love,
The prairie-lawyer, master of us all.

He cannot sleep upon his hillside now.
He is among us:—as in times before!
And we who toss and lie awake for long
Breathe deep, and start, to see him pass the door.

His head is bowed. He thinks on men and kings.
Yes, when the sick world cries, how can he sleep?
Too many peasants fight, they know not why,
Too many homesteads in black terror weep.

The sins of all the war-lords burn his heart.
He sees the dreadnaughts scouring every main.
He carries on his shawl-wrapped shoulders now
The bitterness, the folly and the pain.

He cannot rest until a spirit-dawn
Shall come;—the shining hope of Europe free:
The league of sober folk, the Workers' Earth,
Bringing long peace to Cornland, Alp and Sea.

It breaks his heart that kings must murder still,
That all his hours of travail here for men
Seem yet in vain. And who will bring white peace
That he may sleep upon his hill again?

Euclid

VACHEL LINDSAY

Old Euclid drew a circle
On a sand-beach long ago.
He bounded and enclosed it
With angles thus and so.
His set of solemn graybeards
Nodded and argued much
Of arc and of circumference,
Diameter and such.
A silent child stood by them
From morning until noon
Because they drew such charming
Round pictures of the moon.

Simon Legree—A Negro Sermon

VACHEL LINDSAY

(To be read in your own variety of Negro dialect)

Legree's big house was white and green.
His cotton fields were the best to be seen.
He had strong horses and opulent cattle,
And bloodhounds bold, with chains that would rattle.
His garret was full of curious things:
Books of magic, bags of gold,
And rabbits' feet on long twine strings.
But he went down to the Devil.

Legree he sported a brass-buttoned coat,
A snake-skin necktie, a blood-red shirt,
Legree he had a beard like a goat,
And a thick hairy neck, and eyes like dirt.
His puffed-out cheeks were fish-belly white,
He had great long teeth, and an appetite.
He ate raw meat, 'most every meal,
And rolled his eyes till the cat would squeal.

His fist was an enormous size
To mash poor niggers that told him lies:
He was surely a witch-man in disguise.
But he went down to the Devil.

He wore hip-boots and would wade all day,
To capture his slaves that had fled away.
But he went down to the Devil.

He beat poor Uncle Tom to death
Who prayed for Legree with his last breath.
Then Uncle Tom to Eva flew,
To the high sanctoriums bright and new;
And Simon Legree stared up beneath,
And cracked his heels, and ground his teeth:
And went down to the Devil.

He crossed the yard in the storm and gloom;
He went into his grand front room.
He said, "I killed him, and I don't care."
He kicked a hound, he gave a swear;
He tightened his belt, he took a lamp,
Went down cellar to the webs and damp.
There in the middle of the mouldy floor
He heaved up a slab, he found a door—
And went down to the Devil.

His lamp blew out, but his eyes burned bright.
Simon Legree stepped down all night—
Down, down to the Devil.
Simon Legree he reached the place,
He saw one half of the human race,
He saw the Devil on a wide green throne,
Gnawing the meat from a big ham-bone,
And he said to Mister Devil:

"I see that you have much to eat—
A red ham-bone is surely sweet.
I see that you have lion's feet;
I see your frame is fat and fine,
I see you drink your poison wine—
Blood and burning turpentine."

And the Devil said to Simon Legree:

"I like your style, so wicked and free.
Come sit and share my throne with me,
And let us bark and revel."

And there they sit and gnash their teeth,
And each one wears a hop-vine wreath.
They are matching pennies and shooting craps,
They are playing poker and taking naps.
And old Legree is fat and fine:
He eats the fire, he drinks the wine—
Blood and burning turpentine—
Down, down with the Devil;
Down, down with the Devil;
Down, down with the Devil.

The Leaden-Eyed

VACHEL LINDSAY

Let not young souls be smothered out before
They do quaint deeds and fully flaunt their pride.
It is the world's one crime its babes grow dull,
Its poor are ox-like, limp and leaden-eyed.

Not that they starve, but starve so dreamlessly,
Not that they sow, but that they seldom reap,
Not that they serve, but have no gods to serve,
Not that they die but that they die like sheep.

On the Building of Springfield

VACHEL LINDSAY

Let not our town be large, remembering
That little Athens was the Muses' home,
That Oxford rules the heart of London still,
That Florence gave the Renaissance to Rome.

Record it for the grandson of your son—
A city is not builded in a day:
Our little town cannot complete her soul
Till countless generations pass away.

Now let each child be joined as to a church
To her perpetual hopes, each man ordained:
Let every street be made a reverent aisle
Where Music grows and Beauty is unchained.

Let Science and Machinery and Trade
Be slaves of her, and make her all in all,
Building against our blatant, restless time
An unseen, skilful, medieval wall.

Let every citizen be rich toward God.
Let Christ the beggar, teach divinity.
Let no man rule who holds his money dear.
Let this, our city, be our luxury.

We should build parks that students from afar
Would choose to starve in, rather than go home,
Fair little squares, with Phidian ornament,
Food for the spirit, milk and honeycomb.

Songs shall be sung by us in that good day,
Songs we have written, blood within the rhyme
Beating, as when Old England still was glad,—
The purple, rich Elizabethan time.

* * *

Say, is my prophecy too fair and far?
I only know, unless her faith be high,
The soul of this, our Nineveh, is doomed,
Our little Babylon will surely die.

Some city on the breast of Illinois
No wiser and no better at the start
By faith shall rise redeemed, by faith shall rise
Bearing the western glory in her heart.

The genius of the Maple, Elm and Oak,
The secret hidden in each grain of corn,
The glory that the prairie angels sing
At night when sons of Life and Love are born,

Born but to struggle, squalid and alone,
Broken and wandering in their early years.
When will they make our dusty streets their goal,
Within our attics hide their sacred tears?

When will they start our vulgar blood athrill
With living language, words that set us free?
When will they make a path of beauty clear
Between our riches and our liberty?

We must have many Lincoln-hearted men.
A city is not builded in a day.
And they must do their work, and come and go,
While countless generations pass away.

Factory Windows Are Always Broken

VACHEL LINDSAY

Factory windows are always broken.
Somebody's always throwing bricks,
Somebody's always heaving cinders,
Playing ugly Yahoo tricks.

Factory windows are always broken.
Other windows are let alone.
No one throws through the chapel-window
The bitter, snarling derisive stone.

Factory windows are aways broken.
Something or other is going wrong.
Something is rotten—I think, in Denmark.
End of the factory-window song.

Jesse James

WILLIAM ROSE BENÉT

Jesse James was a two-gun man,
(Roll on, Missouri!)
Strong-arm chief of an outlaw clan.
(From Kansas to Illinois!)
He twirled an old Colt forty-five,
(Roll on, Missouri!)
They never took Jesse James alive.
(Roll, Missouri, roll!)
Jesse James was King of the Wes';
(Cataracks in the Missouri!)
He'd a di'mon' heart in his lef' breas';
(Brown Missouri rolls!)
He'd a fire in his heart no hurt could stifle;
(Thunder, Missouri!)
Lion eyes an' a Winchester rifle.
(Missouri, roll down!)

Jesse James rode a pinto hawse;
Comc at night to a water-cawse;
Tetched with the rowel that pinto's flank;
She sprung the torrent from bank to bank.

Jesse rode through a sleepin' town;
Looked the moonlit street both up an' down;
Crack-crack-crack, the street ran flames
An' a great voice cried, "I'm Jesse James!"

Hawse an' afoot they're after Jess!
(Roll on, Missouri!)
Spurrin' an' spurrin'—but he's gone Wes'.
(Brown Missouri rolls!)
He was ten foot tall when he stood in his boots;
(Lightnin' light the Missouri!)
More'n a match fer sich galoots.
(Roll, Missouri, roll!)

Jesse James rode outa the sage;
Roun' the rocks come the swayin' stage;
Straddlin' the road a giant stan's
An' a great voice bellers, "Throw up yer han's!"

Jesse raked in the di'mon' rings,
The big gold watches an' the yuther things;
Jesse divvied 'em then an' thar
With a cryin' child had lost her mar.

The U. S. Troopers is after Jess;
(Roll on, Missouri!)
Their hawses sweat foam, but he's gone Wes';
(Hear Missouri roar!)
He was broad as a b'ar, he'd a ches' like a drum,
(Wind an' rain through Missouri!)
An' his red hair flamed like Kingdom Come.
(Missouri down to the sea!)

Jesse James all alone in the rain
Stopped an' stuck up the Eas'-boun' train;

Swayed through the coaches with horns an' a tail,
Lit out with the bullion an' the registered mail.

Jess made 'em all turn green with fright,
Quakin' in the aisles in the pitch-black night;
An' he give all the bullion to a pore ole tramp
Campin' nigh the cuttin' in the dirt an' damp.

The whole U. S. is after Jess;
(Roll on, Missouri!)
The son-of-a-gun, if he ain't gone Wes';
(Missouri to the sea!)
He could chaw cold iron an' spit blue flame;
(Cataracks down the Missouri!)
He rode on a catamount he'd larned to tame.
(Hear that Missouri roll!)

Jesse James rode into a bank;
Give his pinto a tetch on the flank;
Jumped the teller's window with an awful crash;
Heaved up the safe an' twirled his mustache;

He said, "So long, boys!" He yelped, "So long!
Feelin' porely to-day—I ain't feelin' strong!"
Rode right through the wall agoin' crack-crack-crack,—
Took the safe home to Mother in a gunny-sack.

They're creepin', they're crawlin', they're stalkin' Jess;
(Roll on, Missouri!)

They's a rumor he's gone much further Wes';
(Roll, Missouri, roll!)
They's word of a cayuse hitched to the bars
(Ruddy clouds on Missouri!)
Of a golden sunset that busts into stars.
(Missouri, roll down!)

Jesse James rode hell fer leather;
He was a hawse an' a man together;
In a cave in a mountain high up in air
He lived with a rattlesnake, a wolf, an' a bear.

Jesse's heart was as sof' as a woman;
Fer guts an' stren'th he was sooper-human;
He could put six shots through a woodpecker's eye
And take in one swaller a gallon o' rye.

They sought him here an' they sought him there,
(Roll on, Missouri!)
But he strides by night through the ways of the air,
(Brown Missouri rolls!)
They say he was took an' they say he is dead;
(Thunder, Missouri!)
But he ain't–he's a sunset overhead!
(Missouri down to the sea!)

Jesse James was a Hercules.
When he went through the woods he tore up the trees
When he went on the plains he smoked the groun'
An' the hull lan' shuddered fer miles aroun'.

Jesse James wore a red bandanner
That waved on the breeze like the Star Spangled Banner;
In seven states he cut up dadoes.
He's gone with the buffler an' the desperadoes.

Yes, Jesse James was a two-gun man
(Roll on, Missouri!)
The same as when this song began;
(From Kansas to Illinois!)
An' when you see a sunset bust into flames
(Lightnin' light the Missouri!)
Or a thunderstorm blaze—that's Jesse James!
(Hear that Missouri roll!)

Last Speech to the Court

BARTOLOMEO VANZETTI

I have talk a great deal of myself
but I even forgot to name Sacco.
Sacco too is a worker,
from his boyhood a skilled worker, lover of work,
with a good job and pay,
a bank account, a good and lovely wife,
two beautiful children and a neat little home
at the verge of a wood, near a brook.

Sacco is a heart, a faith, a character, a man;
a man, lover of nature, and mankind;
a man who gave all, who sacrifice all
to the cause of liberty and to his love for mankind:
money, rest, mundane ambition,
his own wife, his children, himself
and his own life.

Sacco has never dreamt to steal, never to assassinate.
He and I have never brought a morsel
of bread to our mouths, from our childhood to today
which has not been gained by the sweat of our brows.
Never . . .

Oh, yes, I may be more witful, as some have put it;
I am a better babbler than he is, but many, many times

in hearing his heartful voice ringing a faith sublime,
in considering his supreme sacrifice, remembering his
heroism,
I felt small at the presence of his greatness
and found myself compelled to fight back
from my eyes the tears,
and quanch my heart
trobling to my throat to not weep before him:
this man called thief and assassin and doomed.

But Sacco's name will live in the hearts of the people
and in their gratitude when Katzmann's bones
and yours will be dispersed by time;
when your name, his name, your laws, institutions,
and your false god are but a dim rememoring
of a cursed past in which man was wolf
to the man . . .

*

If it had not been for these thing
I might have live out my life
talking at street corners to scorning men.
I might have die, unmarked, unknown, a failure.
Now we are not a failure.
This is our career and our triumph. Never
in our full life could we hope to do such work
for tolerance, for justice, for man's understanding
of man, as now we do by accident.

Our words, our lives, our pains—nothing!
The taking of our lives—lives of a good shoemaker and
  a poor fishpeddler—
all! That last moment belongs to us—
that agony is our triumph.

For St. Bartholomew's Eve

MALCOLM COWLEY

(August 23, 1927)

Then die!
                    Outside the prison gawk
the crowds that you will see no more.
A door slams shut behind you. Walk
with turnkeys down a corridor
smelling of lysol, through the gates
to where a drunken sheriff waits.

St. Nicholas who blessed your birth,
whose hands are rich with gifts, will bear
no further gifts to you on earth,
Sacco, whose heart abounds in prayer
neither to Pilate nor a saint
whose earthly sons die innocent.

And you that would not bow your knee
to God, swarthy Bartholomew,
no God will grant you liberty,
nor Virgin intercede for you,
nor bones of yours make sweet the plot
where governors and judges rot.

A doctor sneezes. A chaplain maps
the routes to heaven. You mount the chair.

A jailor buckles tight the straps
like those which aviators wear.
The surgeon makes a signal.
Die!
lost symbols of our liberty.

Beyond the chair, beyond the bars
of day and night, your path lies free;
yours is an avenue of stars:
march on, O dago Christs, while we
march on to spread your name abroad
like ashes in the winds of God.

The Hill Above the Mine

MALCOLM COWLEY

Nobody comes to the graveyard on the hill,
lost on the blackened slope above the mine,
where coke-oven fumes drift heavily by day
and creeping fires at night; nobody stirs
here by the crumbling wall, where headstones loom
among the blackberry vines; nobody walks
in the blue starlight under the cedar branches
twisted and black against the moon, nor speaks
except the unquiet company of the dead,

and one who calls the roll:
"Ezekiel Cowley?"
Dead.
"Laban and Uriah Evans?"
Dead.
"Jasper McCullough, your three wives, your thirty
children, of whom four bastards?"
Dead, all dead.
"Simon Eliot? Sergeant Danny George?
Judge Peter and Sarah Ellen Farbaugh?"
Dead,
sleeping under the brambles in the starlight
above the unpainted cabins and the mine.

What have you seen, O dead?

"We saw our woods
butchered, flames curling in the maple tops,
white ashes drifting, a railroad in the valley
bridging the creek, and mines under the hill.
We saw our farms lie fallow and houses grow
all summer in the flowerless meadows. Rats
all winter gnawed the last husks in the barn.
In spring the waters rose, crept through the fields
and stripped them bare of soil, while on the hill
we waited and stood firm."

Wait on, O dead!
The waters still shall rise, the hills fold in,
the tombs open to heaven, and you shall ride
eastward on a rain-wind, spurring the thunder,
your white bones drifting like herons across the moon.

The Legion of Iron

LOLA RIDGE

They pass through the great iron gates—
Men with eyes gravely discerning,
Skilled to appraise the tonnage of cranes
Or split an inch into thousandths—
Men tempered by fire as the ore is
And planned to resistance
Like steel that has cooled in the trough;
Silent of purpose, inflexible, set to fulfilment—
To conquer, withstand, overthrow. . . .
Men mannered to large undertakings,
Knowing force as a brother
And power as something to play with,
Seeing blood as a slip of the iron,
To be wiped from the tools
Lest they rust.

But what if they stood aside,
Who hold the earth so careless in the crook of their arms?

What of the flamboyant cities
And the lights guttering out like candles in a wind . . .
And the armies halted. . . .
And the train midway on the mountain
And idle men chaffing across the trenches . . .
And the cursing and lamentation

And the clamor for grain shut in the mills of the world?
What if they stayed apart,
Inscrutably smiling,
Leaving the ground encumbered with dead wire
And the sea to row-boats
And the lands marooned–
Till time should like a paralytic sit,
A mildewed hulk above the nations squatting?

Rhymes from *A Book of Americans*

STEPHEN VINCENT BENÉT
(With Rosemary Benét)

1.

Thomas Jefferson 1743–1826

Thomas Jefferson
What do you say
Under the gravestone
Hidden away?

"I was a giver,
I was a moulder,
I was a builder
With a strong shoulder."

Six feet and over,
Large-boned and ruddy,
The eyes grey-hazel
But bright with study.

The big hands clever
With pen and fiddle
And ready, ever,
For any riddle.

From buying empires,
To planting 'taters,

From Declarations
To trick dumb-waiters.

"I liked the people,
The sweat and crowd of them,
Trusted them always
And spoke aloud of them.

"I liked all learning
And wished to share it
Abroad like pollen
For all who merit.

"I liked queer gadgets
And secret shelves,
And helping nations
To rule themselves."

2.

John Quincy Adams 1767–1848

When President John Quincy
Set out to take a swim,
He'd hang his Presidential clothes
Upon a hickory limb
And bound in the Potomac
Like a dolphin on the swell.
—He was extremely dignified
But rather plump, as well.

And when Supreme Court Justices
Remarked, from a canoe,
"Our Presidents don't do such things."
He merely said, "I do."
He never asked what people thought
But gave them tit for tat.
The Adamses have always been
Remarkably like that.

3.

Daniel Boone 1797–1879

When Daniel Boone goes by at night
The phantom deer arise
And all lost, wild America
Is burning in their eyes.

4.

Abraham Lincoln 1809–1865

Lincoln was a long man.
He liked out of doors.
He liked the wind blowing
And the talk in country stores.

He liked telling stories,
He liked telling jokes.
"Abe's quite a character,"
Said quite a lot of folks.

Lots of folks in Springfield
Saw him every day,
Walking down the street
In his gaunt, long way.

Shawl around his shoulders,
Letters in his hat.
"That's Abe Lincoln."
They thought no more than that.

Knew that he was honest,
Guessed that he was odd,
Knew he had a cross wife
Though she was a Todd.

Knew he had three little boys
Who liked to shout and play,
Knew he had a lot of debts
It took him years to pay.

Knew his clothes and knew his house.
"That's his office, here.
Blame good lawyer on the whole,
Though he's sort of queer.

"Sure, he went to Congress, once,
But he didn't stay.
Can't expect us all to be
Smart as Henry Clay.

"Need a man for troubled times?
Well, I guess we do.
Wonder who we'll ever find?
Yes—I wonder who."

That is how they met and talked,
Knowing and unknowing.
Lincoln was the green pine.
Lincoln kept on growing.

Litany for Dictatorships

STEPHEN VINCENT BENÉT

For all those beaten, for the broken heads,
The fosterless, the simple, the oppressed,
The ghosts in the burning city of our time . . .

For those taken in rapid cars to the house and beaten
By the skilful boys, the boys with the rubber fists,
—Held down and beaten, the table cutting their loins,
Or kicked in the groin and left, with the muscles jerking
Like a headless hen's on the floor of the slaughter-house
While they brought the next man in with his white eyes
staring.
For those who still said "Red Front!" or "God Save the
Crown!"
And for those who were not courageous
But were beaten nevertheless.
For those who spit out the bloody stumps of their teeth
Quietly in the hall,
Sleep well on stone or iron, watch for the time
And kill the guard in the privy before they die,
Those with the deep-socketed eyes and the lamp burning.

For those who carry the scars, who walk lame—for those
Whose nameless graves are made in the prison-yard
And the earth smoothed back before morning and the
lime scattered.

For those slain at once. For those living through months
and years
Enduring, watching, hoping, going each day
To the work or the queue for meat or the secret club,
Living meanwhile, begetting children, smuggling guns,
And found and killed at the end like rats in a drain.

For those escaping
Incredibly into exile and wandering there.
For those who live in the small rooms of foreign cities
And who yet think of the country, the long green grass,
The childhood voices, the language, the way wind smelt
then,
The shape of rooms, the coffee drunk at the table,
The talk with friends, the loved city, the waiter's face,
The gravestones, with the name, where they will not lie
Nor in any of that earth. Their children are strangers.

For those who planned and were leaders and were beaten
And for those, humble and stupid, who had no plan
But were denounced, but grew angry, but told a joke,
But could not explain, but were sent away to the camp,
But had their bodies shipped back in the sealed coffins,
"Died of pneumonia." "Died trying to escape."

For those growers of wheat who were shot by their own
wheat-stacks,
For those growers of bread who were sent to the ice-
locked wastes,
And their flesh remembers their fields.

For those denounced by their smug, horrible children
For a peppermint-star and the praise of the Perfect State,
For all those strangled or gelded or merely starved
To make perfect states; for the priest hanged in his
    cassock,
The Jew with his chest crushed in and his eyes dying,
The revolutionist lynched by the private guards
To make perfect states, in the names of the perfect states.

For those betrayed by the neighbors they shook hands
    with
And for the traitors, sitting in the hard chair
With the loose sweat crawling their hair and their fingers
    restless
As they tell the street and the house and the man's name.

And for those sitting at table in the house
With the lamp lit and the plates and the smell of food,
Talking so quietly; when they hear the cars
And the knock at the door, and they look at each other
    quickly
And the woman goes to the door with a stiff face,
Smoothing her dress.
                        "We are all good citizens here.
We believe in the Perfect State."
                                        And that was the last
Time Tony or Karl or Shorty came to the house
And the family was liquidated later.
It was the last time.

We heard the shots in the night
But nobody knew next day what the trouble was
And a man must go to his work. So I didn't see him
For three days, then, and me near out of my mind
And all the patrols on the streets with their dirty guns
And when he came back, he looked drunk, and the blood was on him.

For the women who mourn their dead in the secret night,
For the children taught to keep quiet, the old children,
The children spat-on at school.
For the wrecked laboratory,
The gutted house, the dunged-picture, the pissed-in well,
The naked corpse of Knowledge flung in the square
And no man lifting a hand and no man speaking.

For the cold of the pistol-butt and the bullet's heat,
For the rope that chokes, the manacles that bind,
The huge voice, metal, that lies from a thousand tubes
And the stuttering machine-gun that answers all.

For the man crucified on the crossed machine-guns
Without name, without resurrection, without stars,
His dark head heavy with death and his flesh long sour
With the smell of his many prisons—John Smith, John Doe,
John Nobody—oh, crack your mind for his name!
Faceless as water, naked as the dust,

Dishonored as the earth the gas-shells poison
And barbarous with portent.
                                        This is he.
This is the man they ate at the green table
Putting their gloves on ere they touch the meat.
This is the fruit of war, the fruit of peace,
The ripeness of invention, the new lamb,
The answer to the wisdom of the wise.
And still he hangs, and still he will not die,
And still, on the steel city of our years
The light fails and the terrible blood streams down.

We thought we were done with these things but we were
    wrong.
We thought, because we had power, we had wisdom.
We thought the long train would run to the end of
    Time.
We thought the light would increase.
Now the long train stands derailed and the bandits loot it.
Now the boar and the asp have power in our time.
Now the night rolls back on the West and the night is
    solid.
Our fathers and ourselves sowed dragon's teeth.
Our children know and suffer the armed men.

Final Autumn

JOSEPHINE W. JOHNSON

End will come swiftly in an early autumn,
Forewarned by blooded rising of the moon,
Its great arc swollen like a hill of fire,
And long continuous lightning in the north,
Portent of that unearthly rain whose knives
Shall slash the hard integument of earth
Down to its unknown core.
And man, having ravaged earth's beauty and outlived
her prime,
Strained from her hands all mystery and dark,
Shall hear
The far wasp-whispering of the flames to come
Over the outworn cities and infertile soil;
Shall know the fierce increasing sound
Of iron cities' great volcanic death,
The roar of oak fire and the straining steel,
The quivering to and fro of towers
Like fiery grass stems in a wind.
And over the broken face of earth shall sear
Iron of the cauterizing flame,
Over the unclean, crying mouths
The clean sound of the flame.

And some men in this hour of death shall know
More heat and glory than had ever come

Into the spare and cautious veins of life,
And cry out with the tardy grief of those who find
Night of a great and unreturning day
In which they had no part.
And some by light of this flame-opened hour
Shall face
The knotted fabric of their lives,
—Woven in darkness and unseen till now,
And will be glad to die.

But there shall be no grief so bitter,
Nor any anguish on the earth that can compare
With the intolerable bitterness of those voices that shall
cry—
Not out of fear of this great tidal flame—
Not for the ashless bodies of the dead,
But out of the knowledge that this burning means
The long ritual of Life brought to a close
In the high horror and red pageantry of Death,
With still the face of God unseen,
His great confessional unread.

The Serf

ROY CAMPBELL

His naked skin clothed in the torrid mist
That puffs in smoke around the patient hooves,
The ploughman drives, a slow somnambulist,
And through the green his crimson furrow grooves.
His heart, more deeply than he wounds the plain,
Long by the rasping share of insult torn,
Red clod, to which the war-cry once was rain
And tribal spears the fatal sheaves of corn,
Lies fallow now. But as the turf divides
I see in the slow progress of his strides
Over the toppled clods and falling flowers,
The timeless, surly patience of the serf
That moves the nearest to the naked earth
And ploughs down palaces, and thrones, and towers.

From *America Remembers*

PAUL ENGLE

Here by this midland lake, the sand-shored water
That pulses with no sea-tide heart, where the grain
Of a nation pauses on its golden way
To the world's belly, and the long trains plunge . . .

*

I remember men, callers
To gods in the gusty rain, to the thunder birds,
Chippers of flint, scratchers of soil thinly
(Now has the earth been torn with the anvil-hammered
Plough deeply for our hunger, and the black shaft sunk).
The trail through the hills was moccasin wide and a
stone
Twisted it, the rivers were swum. *(What of this*
Concrete trampling, the wild arum, the arched bridge?)
The continent lived in its own and eternal way
Dreamless of change.

*

And all
The pulses of the earth were stirred by the pounding
Heart of America and poured their blood
Over the great sea arteries, finding
Sometimes a country like their own, the Finns
By the Minnesota lakes, the Germans over
The prairie farms of Iowa, the English

In the Berkshire hills and valleys. The Southern folk
Left the gay dances, the vineyards mellowed with sun-
light
On the terraced hills, and as Wop and Dago joined
Polack and Bohunk in the towns of steel
Where the great fires burned their guts out—Bethlehem
(O mockery of the little Christ-found village), Gary,
Youngstown, the hard, trip-hammer-beaten names.
The ancient features of the type were changed
Under a different sun, in a clearer air
That entered the lungs like wine, the swarthy face
Paled, cheek bones lifted and narrowed, hair
Straightened and faded, and the body moved
With a lighter step, the toes springy, the eyes
Eager as a bird's, and every man
Had a coiled spring in his nerves that drove him
In a restless fury of life.

The bloods mingled
Madly, the red flame of the sons of men
Who had rowed Ulysses on the wine-dark sea
Burned in the pale blue eyes of the North, eyes hardened
With centuries of staring from Viking masts
Into the unknown oceans—Leif the Lucky
Once beached their dragon-headed prows on the bare
Coast of this land, the first white man. *(Who knows*
What strange multi-fathered child will come
Out of the nervous travail of these bloods
To fashion in a new world continent
A newer breed of men?)

From *The River*

Soundtrack of the Motion Picture

PARE LORENTZ

Black spruce and Norway pine,
Douglas fir and Red cedar,
Scarlet oak and Shagbark hickory.
We built a hundred cities and a thousand towns—
But at what a cost!
We cut the top off the Alleghenies and sent it down the
  river.
We cut the top off Minnesota and sent it down the river.
We cut the top off Wisconsin and sent it down the river.
We left the mountains and the hills slashed and burned,
And moved on.

*

We built a hundred cities and a thousand towns—
But at what a cost!
Poor land makes poor people.
Poor people make poor land.

*

We got the blacks to plant the cotton and they gouged
  the top off the valley.
We got the Swedes to cut the forests, and they sent them
  down the river.

Then we left a hollow-eyed generation to peck at the worn-out valley;
And left the Swedes to shiver in their naked North country.
1903, 1907, 1913, 1922, 1927, 1936, 1937—
For you can't wall out and dam two-thirds the water in the country.
We built dams but the dams filled in.
We built a thousand-mile dyke but it didn't hold;
So we built it higher.
We played with a continent for fifty years.

Flood control? Of the Mississippi?
Control from Denver to Helena;
From Itasca to Paducah;
From Pittsburgh to Cairo—
Control of the wheat, the corn and the cotton land;
Control enough to put back a thousand forests;
Control enough to put the river together again before it is too late . . . before it has picked up the heart of a continent and shoved it into the Gulf of Mexico.

Hope Is a Tattered Flag

CARL SANDBURG

Hope is a tattered flag and a dream out of time.
Hope is a heartspun word, the rainbow, the shadblow in white,
The evening star inviolable over the coal mines,
The shimmer of northern lights across a bitter winter night,
The blue hills beyond the smoke of the steel works,
The birds who go on singing to their mates in peace, war, peace,
The ten-cent crocus bulb blooming in a used-car sales-room,
The horseshoe over the door, the luckpiece in the pocket,
The kiss and the comforting laugh and resolve—
Hope is an echo, hope ties itself yonder, yonder.

The spring grass showing itself where least expected,
The rolling fluff of white clouds on a changeable sky,
The broadcast of strings from Japan, bells from Moscow,
Of the voice of the prime minister of Sweden carried
Across the sea in behalf of a world family of nations
And children singing chorals of the Christ child
And Bach being broadcast from Bethlehem, Pennsyl-vania
And tall skyscrapers practically empty of tenants
And the hands of strong men groping for handholds
And the Salvation Army singing God loves us. . . .

The People, Yes, the People

CARL SANDBURG

The people, yes, the people,
Until the people are taken care of one way or another,
Until the people are solved somehow for the day and hour,
Until then one hears "Yes but the people what about the people?"
Sometimes as though the people is a child to be pleased or fed
Or again a hoodlum you have to be tough with
And seldom as though the people is a caldron and a reservoir
Of the human reserves that shape history,
The river of welcome wherein the broken First Families fade,
The great pool wherein wornout breeds and clans drop for restorative silence.

Fire, chaos, shadows,
Events trickling from a thin line of flame
On into cries and combustions never expected!
The people have the element of surprise.
Where are the kings today?
What has become of their solid and fastened thrones?
Who are the temporary puppets holding sway while anything,

"God only knows what," waits around a corner, sits in the shadows and holds an ax, waiting for the appointed hour?

"The czar has eight million men with guns and bayonets.
"Nothing can happen to the czar.
"The czar is the voice of God and shall live forever.
"Turn and look at the forest of steel and cannon
"Where the czar is guarded by eight million soldiers.
"Nothing can happen to the czar."

They said that for years and in the summer of 1914
In the Year of Our Lord Nineteen Hundred and Fourteen
As a portent and an assurance they said with owl faces:
"Nothing can happen to the czar."
Yet the czar and his bodyguard of eight million vanished
And the czar stood in the cellar before a little firing squad
And the command of fire was given
And the czar stepped into regions of mist and ice
The czar travelled into an ethereal uncharted siberia
While two kaisers also vanished from thrones
Ancient and established in blood and iron—
Two kaisers backed by ten million bayonets
Had their crowns in a gutter, their palaces mobbed.
In fire, chaos, shadows,
In hurricanes beyond foretelling of probabilities,

In the shove and whirl of unforeseen combustions
  The people, yes, the people,
Move eternally in the elements of surprise,
Changing from hammer to bayonet and back to hammer,
The hallelujah chorus forever shifting its star soloists.

Sleep Is a Suspension

CARL SANDBURG

Sleep is a suspension midway
and a conundrum of shadows
lost in the meadows of the moon.
  The people sleep.
  Ai! ai! the people sleep.
Yet the sleepers toss in sleep
and an end comes of sleep
and the sleepers wake.
  Ai! ai! the sleepers wake!

The People Will Live On

CARL SANDBURG

The people will live on.
The learning and blundering people will live on.
They will be tricked and sold and again sold
And go back to the nourishing earth for rootholds,
The people so peculiar in renewal and comeback,
You can't laugh off their capacity to take it.
The mammoth rests between his cyclonic dramas.

The people so often sleepy, weary, enigmatic,
is a vast huddle with many units saying:
"I earn my living.
I make enough to get by
and it takes all my time.
If I had more time
I could do more for myself
and maybe for others.
I could read and study
and talk things over
and find out about things.
It takes time.
I wish I had the time."

The people is a tragic and comic two-face:
hero and hoodlum: phantom and gorilla twisting to moan with a gargoyle mouth: "They

buy me and sell me . . . it's a game . . .
sometime I'll break loose . . ."

Once having marched
Over the margins of animal necessity,
Over the grim line of sheer subsistence
Then man came
To the deeper rituals of his bones,
To the lights lighter than any bones,
To the time for thinking things over,
To the dance, the song, the story,
Or the hours given over to dreaming,
Once having so marched.

Between the finite limitations of the five senses
and the endless yearnings of man for the beyond
the people hold to the humdrum bidding of work and
food
while reaching out when it comes their way
for lights beyond the prison of the five senses,
for keepsakes lasting beyond any hunger or death.
This reaching is alive.
The panderers and liars have violated and smutted it.
Yet this reaching is alive yet
for lights and keepsakes.

The people know the salt of the sea
and the strength of the winds
lashing the corners of the earth.
The people take the earth

as a tomb of rest and a cradle of hope.
Who else speaks for the Family of Man?
They are in tune and step
with constellations of universal law.

The people is a polychrome,
a spectrum and a prism
held in a moving monolith,
a console organ of changing themes,
a clavilux of color poems
wherein the sea offers fog
and the fog moves off in rain
and the labrador sunset shortens
to a nocturne of clear stars
serene over the shot spray
of northern lights.

The steel mill sky is alive.
The fire breaks white and zigzag
shot on a gun-metal gloaming.
Man is a long time coming.
Man will yet win.
Brother may yet line up with brother:

This old anvil laughs at many broken hammers.
There are men who can't be bought.
The fireborn are at home in fire.
The stars make no noise.
You can't hinder the wind from blowing.

Time is a great teacher.
Who can live without hope?
In the darkness with a great bundle of grief
the people march.
In the night, and overhead a shovel of stars for
keeps, the people march:
"Where to? What next?"

PART THREE

A poem should be palpable and mute
As a globed fruit

Dumb
As old medallions to the thumb

Silent as the sleeve-worn stone
Of casement ledges where the moss has grown—

A poem should be wordless
As the flight of birds

* * *

A poem should be motionless in time
As the moon climbs

Leaving, as the moon releases
Twig by twig the night-entangled trees,

Leaving, as the moon behind the winter leaves,
Memory by memory the mind—

A poem should be motionless in time
As the moon climbs

* * *

A poem should be equal to:
Not true

For all the history of grief
An empty doorway and a maple leaf

For love
The leaning grasses and two lights above the sea—

A poem should not mean
But be

—*Archibald MacLeish*

The Return

EZRA POUND

See, they return; ah, see the tentative
Movements, and the slow feet,
The trouble in the pace and the uncertain
Wavering!

See, they return, one, and by one,
With fear, as half-awakened;
As if the snow should hesitate
And murmur in the wind,
        and half turn back;
These were the "Wing'd-with-Awe,"
        Inviolable.

Gods of the wingéd shoe!
With them the silver hounds,
        sniffing the trace of air!

Haie! Haie!
  These were the swift to harry;
These the keen-scented;
These were the souls of blood.

Slow on the leash,
        pallid the leash-men!

The River-Merchant's Wife: A Letter

EZRA POUND

While my hair was still cut straight across my forehead
I played about the front gate, pulling flowers.
You came by on bamboo stilts, playing horse,
You walked about my seat, playing with blue plums.
And we went on living in the village of Chokan:
Two small people, without dislike or suspicion.

At fourteen I married My Lord you.
I never laughed, being bashful.
Lowering my head, I looked at the wall.
Called to, a thousand times, I never looked back.

At fifteen I stopped scowling,
I desired my dust to be mingled with yours
Forever and forever and forever.
Why should I climb the look out?

At sixteen you departed,
You went into far Ku-to-yen, by the river of swirling
 eddies,
And you have been gone five months.
The monkeys make sorrowful noise overhead.

You dragged your feet when you went out.
By the gate now, the moss is grown, the different mosses,

Too deep to clear them away!
The leaves fall early this autumn, in wind.
The paired butterflies are already yellow with August
Over the grass in the West garden;
They hurt me. I grow older.
If you are coming down through the narrows of the river Kiang,
Please let me know beforehand,
And I will come out to meet you
As far as Cho-fu-Sa.

(From the Chinese of Rihaku.)

Canto XVII

EZRA POUND

So that the vines burst from my fingers
And the bees weighted with pollen
Move heavily in the vine-shoots:
    chirr—chirr—chir-rikk—a purring sound,
And the birds sleepily in the branches.
    ZAGREUS! IO ZAGREUS!
With the first pale-clear of the heaven
And the cities set in their hills,
And the goddess of the fair knees
Moving there, with the oak-woods behind her,
The green slope, with white hounds
        leaping about her;
And thence down to the creek's mouth, until evening,
Flat water before me,
    and the trees growing in water,
Marble trunks out of stillness,
On past the palazzi,
                    in the stillness,
The light now, not of the sun.
                    Chrysophrase,
And the water green clear, and blue clear;
On, to the great cliffs of amber.
                            Between them,
Cave of Nerea,
  she like a great shell curved,

And the boat drawn without sound,
Without odour of ship-work,
Nor bird-cry, nor any noise of wave moving,
Nor splash of porpoise, nor any noise of wave moving,
Within her cave, Nerea,
                                        she like a great shell curved
In the suavity of the rock,
                                          cliff green-gray in the far,
In the near, the gate-cliffs of amber,
And the wave
                        green clear, and blue clear,
And the cave salt-white, and glare-purple,
            cool, porphyry smooth,
            the rock sea-worn.
No gull-cry, no sound of porpoise,
Sand as of malachite, and no cold there,
         the light not of the sun.

Zagreus, feeding his panthers,
         the turf clear as on hills under light.
And under the almond-trees, gods,
         with them, *choros nympharum*. Gods,
Hermes and Athene,
                                   As shaft of compass,
Between them, trembled—
To the left is the place of fauns,
                          sylva nympharum;
The low wood, moor-scrub,
      the doe, the young spotted deer,

leap up through the broom-plants,
as dry leaf amid yellow.
And by one cut of the hills,
the great alley of Memnons.
Beyond sea, crests seen over dune
Night sea churning shingle,
To the left, the alley of cypress.
A boat came,
One man holding her sail,
Guiding her with oar caught over gunwale, saying:
" There, in the forest of marble,
" the stone trees—out of water—
" the arbours of stone—
" marble leaf, over leaf,
" silver, steel over steel,
" silver beaks rising and crossing,
" prow set against prow,
" stone, ply over ply,
" the gilt beams flare of an evening"
Borso, Carmagnola, the men of craft, *i vitrei,*
Thither at one time, time after time,
And the waters richer than glass,
Bronze gold, the blaze over the silver,
Dye-pots in the torch-light,
The flash of wave under prows,
And the silver beaks rising and crossing.
Stone trees, white and rose-white in the darkness,
Cypress there by the towers,
Drift under hulls in the night.

"In the gloom the gold
Gathers the light about it." . . .

Now supine in burrow, half over-arched bramble,
One eye for the sea, through that peek-hole,
Gray light, with Athene.
Zothar and her elephants, the gold loin-cloth,
The sistrum, shaken, shaken,
        the cohorts of her dancers.
And Aletha, by bend of the shore,
        with her eyes seaward,
    and in her hands sea-wrack
Salt-bright with the foam.
Koré through the bright meadow,
        with green-gray dust in the grass:
"For this hour, brother of Circe."
Arm laid over my shoulder,
Saw the sun for three days, the sun fulvid,
As a lion lift over sand-plain;
                                        and that day,
And for three days, and none after,
Splendour, as the splendour of Hermes,
And shipped thence
                                to the stone place,
Pale white, over water,
                                known water,
And the white forest of marble, bent bough over bough,
The pleached arbour of stone,

Thither Borso, when they shot the barbed arrow at him,
And Carmagnola, between the two columns,
Sigismundo, after that wreck in Dalmatia,
    Sunset like the grasshopper flying.

my sweet old etcetera

E. E. CUMMINGS

my sweet old etcetera
aunt lucy during the recent

war could and what
is more did tell you just
what everybody was fighting

for,
my sister

isabel created hundreds
(and
hundreds) of socks not to
mention shirts fleaproof earwarmers

etcetera wristers etcetera, my
mother hoped that

i would die etcetera
bravely of course my father used
to become hoarse talking about how it was
a privilege and if only he
could meanwhile my

self etcetera lay quietly
in the deep mud et

cetera
(dreaming,
et
  cetera, of
Your smile
eyes knees and of your Etcetera)

Paris; this April sunset completely utters

E. E. CUMMINGS

Paris;this April sunset completely utters
utters serenely silently a cathedral

before whose upward lean magnificent face
the streets turn young with rain,

spiral acres of bloated rose
coiled within cobalt miles of sky
yield to and heed
the mauve
　　　　of twilight(who slenderly descends,
daintily carrying in her eyes the dangerous first stars)
people move love hurry in a gently

arriving gloom and
see!(the new moon
fills abruptly with sudden silver
these torn pockets of lame and begging colour)while
there and here the lithe indolent prostitute
Night,argues

with certain houses

i go to this window

E. E. CUMMINGS

i go to this window

just as day dissolves
when it is twilight(and
looking up in fear

i see the new moon
thinner than a hair)

making me feel
how myself has been coarse and dull
compared with you,silently who are
and cling
to my mind always

But now she sharpens and becomes crisper
until i smile with knowing
—and all about
herself

the sprouting largest final air

plunges
            inward with hurled
downward thousands of enormous dreams

impossibly, motivated by midnight

E. E. CUMMINGS

impossibly

motivated by midnight
the flyspecked abdominous female
indubitably tellurian
strolls
        emitting minute grins

each an intaglio.
Nothing
has also carved upon her much

too white forehead a pair of
eyes which mutter thickly(as one merely
terriculous American an instant doubts
the authenticity

of these antiquities–relaxing
                                                hurries

elsewhere;to blow

incredible wampum

if i have made, my lady, intricate

E. E. CUMMINGS

if i have made,my lady,intricate
imperfect various things chiefly which wrong
your eyes(frailer than most deep dreams are frail)
songs less firm than your body's whitest song
upon my mind–if I have failed to snare
the glance too shy–if through my singing slips
the very skillful strangeness of your smile
the keen primeval silence of your hair

–let the world say "his most wise music stole
nothing from death"–
                                        you only will create
(who are so perfectly alive)my shame:
lady through whose profound and fragile lips
the sweet small clumsy feet of April came

into the ragged meadow of my soul.

The Hippopotamus

T. S. ELIOT

And when this epistle is read among you, cause that it be read also in the church of the Laodiceans.

The broad-backed hippopotamus
Rests on his belly in the mud;
Although he seems so firm to us
He is merely flesh and blood.

Flesh-and-blood is weak and frail,
Susceptible to nervous shock;
While the True Church can never fail
For it is based upon a rock.

The hippo's feeble steps may err
In compassing material ends,
While the True Church need never stir
To gather in its dividends.

The 'potamus can never reach
The mango on the mango-tree;
But fruits of pomegranate and peach
Refresh the Church from over sea.

At mating time the hippo's voice
Betrays inflexions hoarse and odd,
But every week we hear rejoice
The Church, at being one with God.

The hippopotamus's day
Is passed in sleep; at night he hunts;
God works in a mysterious way—
The Church can sleep and feed at once.

I saw the 'potamus take wing
Ascending from the damp savannas,
And quiring angels round him sing
The praise of God, in loud hosannas.

Blood of the lamb shall wash him clean
And him shall heavenly arms enfold,
Among the saints he shall be seen
Performing on a harp of gold.

He shall be washed as white as snow,
By all the martyr'd virgins kist,
While the True Church remains below
Wrapt in the old miasmal mist.

Gerontion

T. S. ELIOT

> *Thou hast nor youth nor age*
> *But as it were an after dinner sleep*
> *Dreaming of both.*

Here I am, an old man in a dry month,
Being read to by a boy, waiting for rain.
I was neither at the hot gates
Nor fought in the warm rain
Nor knee deep in the salt marsh, heaving a cutlass,
Bitten by flies, fought.
My house is a decayed house,
And the Jew squats on the window sill, the owner,
Spawned in some estaminet of Antwerp,
Blistered in Brussels, patched and peeled in London,
The goat coughs at night in the field overhead;
Rocks, moss, stonecrop, iron, merds.
The woman keeps the kitchen, makes tea,
Sneezes at evening, poking the peevish gutter.

I an old man,
A dull head among windy spaces.

Signs are taken for wonders. "We would see a sign!"
The word within a word, unable to speak a word,
Swaddled with darkness. In the juvescence of the year
Came Christ the tiger.

In depraved May, dogwood and chestnut, flowering judas,
To be eaten, to be divided, to be drunk
Among whispers; by Mr. Silvero
With caressing hands, at Limoges
Who walked all night in the next room;

By Hakagawa, bowing among the Titians;
By Madame de Tornquist, in the dark room
Shifting the candles; Fraulein von Kulp
Who turned in the hall, one hand on the door. Vacant
  shuttles
Weave the wind. I have no ghosts,
An old man in a draughty house
Under a windy knob.

After such knowledge, what forgiveness? Think now
History has many cunning passages, contrived corridors
And issues, deceives with whispering ambitions,
Guides us by vanities. Think now
She gives when our attention is distracted
And what she gives, gives with such supple confusions
That the giving famishes the craving. Gives too late
What's not believed in, or if still believed,
In memory only, reconsidered passion. Gives too soon
Into weak hands, what's thought can be dispensed with
Till the refusal propagates a fear. Think
Neither fear nor courage saves us. Unnatural vices
Are fathered by our heroism. Virtues

Are forced upon us by our impudent crimes.
These tears are shaken from the wrath-bearing tree.

The tiger springs in the new year. Us he devours. Think
  at last
We have not reached conclusion, when I
Stiffen in a rented house. Think at last
I have not made this show purposelessly
And it is not by any concitation
Of the backward devils.
I would meet you upon this honestly.
I that was near your heart was removed therefrom
To lose beauty in terror, terror in inquisition.
I have lost my passion: why should I need to keep it
Since what is kept must be adulterated?
I have lost my sight, smell, hearing, taste and touch:
How should I use them for your closer contact?

These with a thousand small deliberations
Protract the profit, of their chilled delirium,
Excite the membrane, when the sense has cooled,
With pungent sauces, multiply variety
In a wilderness of mirrors. What will the spider do,
Suspend its operations, will the weevil
Delay? De Bailhache, Fresca, Mrs. Cammell, whirled
Beyond the circuit of the shuddering Bear
In fractured atoms. Gull against the wind, in the windy
  straits

Of Belle Isle, or running on the Horn,
White feathers in the snow, the Gulf claims,
And an old man driven by the Trades
To a sleepy corner.

Tenants of the house,
Thoughts of a dry brain in a dry season.

The Hollow Men

T. S. ELIOT

A penny for the Old Guy

I

We are the hollow men
We are the stuffed men
Leaning together
Headpiece filled with straw. Alas!
Our dried voices, when
We whisper together
Are quiet and meaningless
As wind in dry grass
Or rats' feet over broken glass
In our dry cellar

Shape without form, shade without colour,
Paralyzed force, gesture without motion;

Those who have crossed
With direct eyes, to death's other Kingdom
Remember us–if at all–not as lost
Violent souls, but only
As the hollow men
The stuffed men.

II

Eyes I dare not meet in dreams
In death's dream kingdom
These do not appear:
There, the eyes are
Sunlight on a broken column
There, is a tree swinging
And voices are
In the wind's singing
More distant and more solemn
Than a fading star.

Let me be no nearer
In death's dream kingdom
Let me also wear
Such deliberate disguises
Rat's coat, crowskin, crossed staves
In a field
Behaving as the wind behaves
No nearer–

Not that final meeting
In the twilight kingdom

III

This is the dead land
This is cactus land
Here the stone images
Are raised, here they receive

The supplication of a dead man's hand
Under the twinkle of a fading star.

Is it like this
In death's other kingdom
Waking alone
At the hour when we are
Trembling with tenderness
Lips that would kiss
Form prayers to broken stone.

IV

The eyes are not here
There are no eyes here
In this valley of dying stars
In this hollow valley
This broken jaw of our lost kingdoms

In this last of meeting places
We grope together
And avoid speech
Gathered on this beach of the tumid river

Sightless, unless
The eyes reappear
As the perpetual star
Multifoliate rose
Of death's twilight kingdom
The hope only
Of empty men.

V

Here we go round the prickly pear
Prickly pear prickly pear
Here we go round the prickly pear
At five o'clock in the morning.

Between the idea
And the reality
Between the motion
And the act
Falls the Shadow

For Thine is the Kingdom

Between the conception
And the creation
Between the emotion
And the response
Falls the Shadow

Life is very long

Between the desire
And the spasm
Between the potency
And the existence
Between the essence
And the descent
Falls the Shadow

For Thine is the Kingdom

For Thine is
Life is
For Thine is the

This is the way the world ends
This is the way the world ends
This is the way the world ends
Not with a bang but a whimper.

From *The Rock*

T. S. ELIOT

The Eagle soars in the summit of Heaven,
The Hunter with his dogs pursues his circuit,
O perpetual revolution of configured stars,
O perpetual recurrence of determined seasons,
O world of spring and autumn, birth and dying!
The endless cycle of idea and action,
Endless invention, endless experiment,
Brings knowledge of motion, but not of stillness;
Knowledge of speech, but not of silence;
Knowledge of words, and ignorance of the Word.
All our knowledge brings us nearer to our ignorance,
All our ignorance brings us nearer to death,
But nearness to death no nearer to God.
Where is the Life we have lost in living?
Where is the wisdom we have lost in knowledge?
Where is the knowledge we have lost in information?
The cycles of Heaven in twenty centuries
Bring us farther from God and nearer to the Dust.
I journey to London, to the timekept City,
Where the River flows, with foreign flotations.
There I was told: we have too many churches,
And too few chop-houses. There I was told
Let the vicars retire. Men do not need the Church
In the place where they work, but where they spend
  their Sundays.

In the City, we need no bells:
Let them waken the suburbs.
I journeyed to the suburbs, and there I was told:
We toil for six days, on the seventh we must motor
To Hindhead, or Maidenhead.
If the weather is foul we stay at home and read the
  papers,
In industrial districts, there I was told
Of economic laws.
In the pleasant countryside, there it seemed
That the country now is only fit for picnics.
And the church does not seem to be wanted
In country or in suburb; and in the town
Only for important weddings.

In Time Like Glass

WALTER JAMES TURNER

In Time like glass the stars are set,
And seeming-fluttering butterflies
Are fixéd fast in Time's glass net
With mountains and with maids' bright eyes.

Above the cold Cordilleras hung
The wingéd eagle and the Moon:
The gold, snow-throated orchid sprung
From gloom where peers the dark baboon:

The Himalayas' white, rapt brows;
The jewel-eyed bear that threads their caves;
The lush plains' lowing herds of cows;
That Shadow entering human graves:

All these like stars in Time are set,
They vanish but can never pass;
The Sun that with them fades is yet
Fast-fixed as they in Time like glass.

Peter Quince at the Clavier

WALLACE STEVENS

I

Just as my fingers on these keys
Make music, so the self-same sounds
On my spirit make a music too.

Music is feeling then, not sound;
And thus it is that what I feel,
Here in this room, desiring you,

Thinking of your blue-shadowed silk,
Is music. It is like the strain
Waked in the elders by Susanna:

Of a green evening, clear and warm,
She bathed in her still garden, while
The red-eyed elders, watching, felt

The basses of their being throb
In witching chords, and their thin blood
Pulse pizzicati of Hosanna.

II

In the green evening, clear and warm,
Susanna lay.
She searched
The touch of springs,

And found
Concealed imaginings.
She sighed
For so much melody.

Upon the bank she stood
In the cool
Of spent emotions.
She felt, among the leaves,
The dew
Of old devotions.

She walked upon the grass,
Still quavering.
The winds were like her maids,
On timid feet,
Fetching her woven scarves,
Yet wavering.

A breath upon her hand
Muted the night.
She turned—
A cymbal clashed,
And roaring horns.

III

Soon, with a noise like tambourines,
Came her attendant Byzantines.

They wondered why Susanna cried
Against the elders by her side:

And as they whispered, the refrain
Was like a willow swept by rain.

Anon their lamps' uplifted flame
Revealed Susanna and her shame.

And then the simpering Byzantines,
Fled, with a noise like tambourines.

IV

Beauty is momentary in the mind—
The fitful tracing of a portal;
But in the flesh it is immortal.

The body dies; the body's beauty lives.
So evenings die, in their green going,
A wave, interminably flowing.

So gardens die, their meek breath scenting
The cowl of Winter, done repenting.
So maidens die to the auroral
Celebration of a maiden's choral.

Susanna's music touched the bawdy strings
Of those white elders; but, escaping,
Left only Death's ironic scraping.
Now in its immortality, it plays
On the clear viol of her memory,
And makes a constant sacrament of praise.

The Mechanical Optimist

WALLACE STEVENS

A lady dying of diabetes
Listened to the radio,
Catching the lesser dithyrambs.
So heaven collects its bleating lambs.

Her useless bracelets fondly fluttered,
Paddling the melodic swirls,
The idea of god no longer sputtered
At the roots of her indifferent curls.

The idea of the Alps grew large,
Not yet, however, a thing to die in.
It seemed serener just to die,
To float off on the floweriest barge,

Accompanied by the exegesis
Of familiar things in a cheerful voice,
Like the night before Christmas and all the carols.
Dying lady, rejoice, rejoice!

Sunday Morning Apples

HART CRANE

To William Sommer, Painter

The leaves will fall again sometime and fill
The fleece of nature with those purposes
That are your rich and faithful strength of line.

But now there are challenges to spring
In that ripe nude with head
reared
Into a realm of swords, her purple shadow
Bursting on the winter of the world
From whiteness that cries defiance to the snow.

A boy runs with a dog before the sun, straddling
Spontaneities that form their independent orbits,
Their own perennials of light
In the valley where you live
(called Brandywine).

I have seen the apples there that toss you secrets,—
Beloved apples of seasonable madness
That feed your inquiries with aerial wine.

Put them again beside a pitcher with a knife,
And poise them full and ready for explosion—
The apples, Bill, the apples!

Emblems of Conduct

HART CRANE

By a peninsula the wanderer sat and sketched
The uneven valley graves. While the apostle gave
Alms to the meek the volcano burst
With sulphur and aureate rocks . . .
For joy rides in stupendous coverings
Luring the living into spiritual gates.

Orators follow the universe
And radio the complete laws to the people.
The apostle conveys thought through discipline.
Bowls and cups fill historians with adorations,—
Dull lips commemorating spiritual gates.

The wanderer later chose this spot of rest
Where marble clouds support the sea
And where was finally borne a chosen hero.
By that time summer and smoke were past.
Dolphins still played, arching the horizons,
But only to build memories of spiritual gates.

Black Tambourine

HART CRANE

The interests of a black man in a cellar
Mark tardy judgment on the world's closed door.
Gnats toss in the shadow of a bottle,
And a roach spans a crevice in the floor.

Æsop, driven to pondering, found
Heaven with the tortoise and the hare;
Fox brush and sow ear top his grave
And mingling incantations on the air.

The black man, forlorn in the cellar,
Wanders in some mid-kingdom, dark, that lies
Between his tambourine, stuck on the wall,
And, in Africa, a carcass quick with flies.

Voyages II

HART CRANE

—And yet this great wink of eternity,
Of rimless floods, unfettered leewardings,
Samite sheeted and processioned where
Her undinal vast belly moonward bends,
Laughing the wrapt inflections of our love;

Take this Sea, whose diapason knells
On scrolls of silver snowy sentences,
The sceptred terror of whose sessions rends
As her demeanors motion well or ill,
All but the pieties of lovers' hands.

And onward, as bells off San Salvador
Salute the crocus lustres of the stars,
In these poinsettia meadows of her tides,—
Adagios of islands, O my Prodigal,
Complete the dark confessions her veins spell.

Mark how her turning shoulders wind the hours,
And hasten while her penniless rich palms
Pass superscription of bent foam and wave,—
Hasten, while they are true,—sleep, death, desire,
Close round one instant in one floating flower.

Bind us in time, O Seasons clear, and awe.
O minstrel galleons of Carib fire,
Bequeath us to no earthly shore until
Is answered in the vortex of our grave
The seal's wide spindrift gaze toward paradise.

From *The Bridge*

HART CRANE

The River

. . . and past
the din and slogans
of the year—

Stick your patent name on a signboard
brother—all over—going west—young man
Tintex—Japalac—Certain-teed Overalls ads
and lands sakes! under the new playbill ripped
in the guaranteed corner—see Bert Williams what?
Minstrels when you steal a chicken just
save me the wing for if it isn't
Erie it ain't for miles around a
Mazda—and the telegraphic night coming on Thomas

a Ediford—and whistling down the tracks
a headlight rushing with the sound—can you
imagine—while an EXpress makes time like
SCIENCE—COMMERCE and the HOLYGHOST
RADIO ROARS IN EVERY HOME WE HAVE THE
NORTHPOLE
WALLSTREET AND VIRGINBIRTH WITHOUT
STONES OR
WIRES OR EVEN RUNning brooks connecting ears
and no more sermons windows flashing roar
breathtaking—as you like it . . . eh?

So the 20th Century—so
whizzed the Limited—roared by and left
three men, still hungry on the tracks, ploddingly
watching the tail lights wizen and converge, slipping gimleted and neatly out of sight.

*

to those
whose addresses
are never near

The last bear, shot drinking in the Dakotas
Loped under wires that span the mountain stream.
Keen instruments, strung to a vast precision
Bind town to town and dream to ticking dream.
But some men take their liquor slow—and count
—Though they'll confess no rosary nor clue—
The river's minute by the far brook's year.
Under a world of whistles, wires and steam
Caboose-like they go ruminating through
Ohio, Indiana—blind baggage—
To Cheyenne tagging . . . Maybe Kalamazoo.

Time's rendings, time's blendings they construe
As final reckonings of fire and snow;
Strange bird-wit, like the elemental gist
Of unwalled winds they offer, singing low
My Old Kentucky Home and *Casey Jones,*
Some Sunny Day. I heard a road-gang chanting so.
And afterwards, who had a colt's eyes—one said,
"Jesus! Oh I remember watermelon days!" And sped

High in a cloud of merriment, recalled
"—And when my Aunt Sally Simpson smiled," he drawled—
"It was almost Louisiana, long ago."
"There's no place like Booneville though, Buddy,"
One said, excising a last burr from his vest,
"—For early trouting." Then peering in the can,
"—But I kept on the tracks." Possessed, resigned,
He trod the fire down pensively and grinned,
Spreading dry shingles of a beard. . . .
Behind
My father's cannery works I used to see
Rail-squatters ranged in nomad raillery,
The ancient men—wifeless or runaway
Hobo-trekkers that forever search
An empire wilderness of freight and rails.
Each seemed a child, like me, on a loose perch,
Holding to childhood like some termless play.
John, Jake or Charley, hopping the slow freight
—Memphis to Tallahassee—riding the rods,
Blind fists of nothing, humpty-dumpty clods.

but who have
touched her, knowing
her without name

Yet they touch something like a key perhaps.
From pole to pole across the hills, the states
—They know a body under the wide rain;
Youngsters with eyes like fjords, old reprobates

With racetrack jargon,—dotting immensity
They lurk across her, knowing her yonder breast
Snow-silvered, sumac-stained or smoky blue—
Is past the valley-sleepers, south or west.
—As I have trod the rumorous midnights, too,

And past the circuit of the lamp's thin flame
(O Nights that brought me to her body bare!)
Have dreamed beyond the print that bound her name.
Trains sounding the long blizzards out—I heard
Wail into distances I knew were hers.
Papooses crying on the wind's long mane
Screamed redskin dynasties that fled the brain,
—Dead echoes! But I knew her body there,
Time like a serpent down her shoulder, dark,
And space, an eaglet's wing, laid on her hair.

nor the myths
of her fathers . . .

Under the Ozarks, domed by Iron Mountain,
The old gods of the rain lie wrapped in pools
Where eyeless fish curvet a sunken fountain
And re-descend with corn from querulous crows.
Such pilferings make up their timeless eatage,
Propitiate them for their timber torn
By iron, iron—always the iron dealt cleavage!
They doze now, below axe and powder horn.

And Pullman breakfasters glide glistening steel
From tunnel into field—iron strides the dew—

Straddles the hill, a dance of wheel on wheel.
You have a half-hour's wait at Siskiyou,
Or stay the night and take the next train through.
Southward, near Cairo passing, you can see
The Ohio merging,—borne down Tennessee;
And if it's summer and the sun's in dusk
Maybe the breeze will lift the River's musk
—As though the waters breathed that you might know
Memphis Johnny, Steamboat Bill, Missouri Joe.
Oh, lean from the window, if the train slows down,
As though you touched hands with some ancient clown,
—A little while gaze absently below
And hum *Deep River* with them while they go.

Yes, turn again and sniff once more—look see,
O Sheriff, Brakeman and Authority—
Hitch up your pants and crunch another quid,
For you, too, feed the River timelessly.
And few evade full measure of their fate;
Always they smile out eerily what they seem.
I could believe he joked at heaven's gate—
Dan Midland—jolted from the cold brake-beam.

Down, down—born pioneers in time's despite,
Grimed tributaries to an ancient flow—
They win no frontier by their wayward plight,
But drift in stillness, as from Jordan's brow.

You will not hear it as the sea; even stone
Is not more hushed by gravity . . . But slow,
As loth to take more tribute—sliding prone
Like one whose eyes were buried long ago

The River, spreading, flows—and spends your dream.
What are you, lost within this tideless spell?
You are your father's father, and the stream—
A liquid theme that floating niggers swell.

Damp tonnage and alluvial march of days—
Nights turbid, vascular with silted shale
And roots surrendered down of moraine clays:
The Mississippi drinks the farthest dale.

O quarrying passion, undertowed sunlight!
The basalt surface drags a jungle grace
Ochreous and lynx-barred in lengthening might;
Patience! and you shall reach the biding place!

Over De Soto's bones the freighted floors
Throb past the City storied of three thrones.
Down two more turns the Mississippi pours
(Anon tall ironsides up from salt lagoons)

And flows within itself, heaps itself free.
All fades but one thin skyline 'round . . . Ahead
No embrace opens but the stinging sea;
The River lifts itself from its long bed,

Poised wholly on its dream, a mustard glow
Tortured with history, its one will—flow!
—The Passion spreads in wide tongues, choked and slow,
Meeting the Gulf, hosannas silently below.

Purgatorio

HART CRANE

My country, O my land, my friends—
Am I apart—here from you in a land
Where all your gas lights—faces—sputum gleam
Like something left, forsaken—here am I—
And are these stars—the high plateau—the scents
Of Eden and the dangerous tree—are these
The landscape of confession—and if confession
So absolution? Wake pines—but pines wake here.
I dream the too-keen cider—the too-soft snow.
Where are the bayonets that the scorpion may not grow?
Here quakes of earth make houses fall—
And all my countrymen I see rush toward one stall;
Exile is thus purgatory—not such as Dante built,

But rather like a blanket than a quilt,
And I have no decision—is it green or brown
That I prefer to country or to town?
I am unraveled, umbilical anew,
As ring the church bells here in Mexico—
(They ring too obdurately here to heed my call)
And what hours they forget to chime I'll know,
As one whose altitude at one time, was not so.

Here Lies a Lady

JOHN CROWE RANSOM

Here lies a lady of beauty and high degree.
Of chills and fever she died, of fever and chills,
The delight of her husband, her aunts, and infant of
three,
And of medicos marvelling sweetly on her ills.

For either she burned, and her confident eyes would
blaze,
And her fingers fly in a manner to puzzle their heads—
What was she making? Why, nothing; she sat in a maze
Of old scraps of laces, snipped into curious shreds—

Or this would pass, and the light of her fire decline
Till she lay discouraged and cold as a thin stalk white
and blown,
And would not open her eyes, to kisses, to wine;
The sixth of these states was her last; the cold settled
down.

Sweet ladies, long may ye bloom, and toughly I hope ye
may thole,
But was she not lucky? In flowers and lace and mourning,
In love and great honour we bade God rest her soul
After six little spaces of chill, and six of burning.

Prelude LVI

CONRAD AIKEN

Rimbaud and Verlaine, precious pair of poets,
Genius in both (but what is genius?) playing
Chess on a marble table at an inn
With chestnut blossom falling in blond beer
And on their hair and between knight and bishop—
Sunlight squared between them on the chess-board
Cirrus in heaven, and a squeal of music
Blown from the leathern door of Ste. Sulpice—

Discussing, between moves, iamb and spondee
Anacoluthon and the open vowel
God the great peacock with his angel peacocks
And his dependent peacocks the bright stars:
Disputing too of fate as Plato loved it,
Or Sophocles, who hated and admired,
Or Socrates, who loved and was amused:

Verlaine puts down his pawn upon a leaf
And closes his long eyes, which are dishonest,
And says 'Rimbaud, there is one thing to do:
We must take rhetoric, and wring its neck! . . .'
Rimbaud considers gravely, moves his Queen;
And then removes himself to Timbuctoo.

And Verlaine dead,—with all his jades and mauves;
And Rimbaud dead in Marseilles with a vision,
His leg cut off, as once before his heart;
And all reported by a later lackey,
Whose virtue is his tardiness in time.

Let us describe the evening as it is:—
The stars disposed in heaven as they are:
Verlaine and Shakespeare rotting, where they rot,
Rimbaud remembered, and too soon forgot;

Order in all things, logic in the dark;
Arrangement in the atom and the spark;
Time in the heart and sequence in the brain—

Such as destroyed Rimbaud and fooled Verlaine
And let us then take godhead by the neck—
And strangle it, and with it, rhetoric.

Idiot

ALLEN TATE

The idiot greens the meadows with his eyes,
The meadow creeps implacable and still;
A dog barks, the hammock swings, he lies.
One two three the cows bulge on the hill.

Motion that is not time erects snowdrifts
While sister's hand sieves waterfalls of lace.
With a palm fan closer than death he lifts
Thc Ozarks and tilted seas across his face.

In the long sunset where impatient sound
Strips niggers to a multiple of backs
Flies yield their heat, magnolias drench the ground
With Appomattox! The shadows lie in stacks.

The julep glass weaves echoes in Jim's kinks
While ashy Jim puts murmurs in the day:
Now in the idiot's heart a chamber stinks
Of dead asters, as the potter's field of May.

All evening the marsh is a slick pool
Where dream wild hares, witch hazel, pretty girls.
"Up from the important picnic of a fool
Those rotted asters!" Eddy on eddy swirls

The innocent mansion of a panther's heart!
It crumbles, tick-tick time drags it in
Till now his arteries lag and now they start
Reverence with the frigid gusts of sin—

The stillness pelts the eye, assaults the hair;
A beech sticks out a branch to warm the stars,
A lightning-bug jerks angles in the air,
Diving. "I am the captain of new wars!"

The dusk runs down the lane driven like hail;
Far off a precise whistle is escheat
To the dark; and then the towering weak and pale
Covers his eyes with memory like a sheet.

A Hymn to No One Body

JAMES PALMER WADE

On a winter evening, by a winter fire
And a friend whose stormy winter is now grown
Complete (sometimes I think that I shall tire
Of rehearsing this thing; stone by stone

Of my heart drawn out and put back); well, we sat
And talked despairingly and drank our tea.
My thoughts flew by; his thoughts were this or that.
He would not look at me

As the fire dashed past its ashes and I cried
Out to him, scarcely knowing why,
And saying nothing, nothing. His eyes lied
At hearing for the street-car going by.

Ah, Doctor Eyes-and-Glasses, you know
How to read with expression and some mind,
But back of that your selves vaguely blow,
And we others go on outside blind.

On a winter evening by a winter fire,
We sat together at casuistry of heart.
We were not friends. We stormed meagerly there
To feel our minor selves in a minor part.

We stood up. His forehead had turned white;
I could not see his eyes. We got our hats
And coats and spoke of Mexico. "Goodnight,"
We said, and the night emptied of flats.

Stores, churches, pounding footsteps, and his pale
Regard shook by me. Only the fog carried there
The minor nose, the crepe hair learnèd and stale,
That scattered the night and left me standing here
An old man mumbling out an old man's dreary tale,
In a quiet house beside a quiet street
Of the incredible city of our defeat.

From *The Jungle*

ARCHIBALD FLEMING

Report

. . . Until, finally,
After aching, laming stages they came at last
To the swift intensity of the jumping-off place:
Boys yelled shifting boxes, their palms
Slippery with sweat, to the belling of orders
In noon's-brass furnace; confusion,
Collisions and cursing, the sun's anger
Focused in strange phonetics; men went down
Stooping with heat and their loads to the river,
Clanging equipment and tins of dried food in the boats,
Cameras, cartridges, bolt-action rifles,
Instruments, microscopes, slide-covers, slides,
Nets, bottles, medicines, and dissecting tools.
Jogged by a hypodermic anticipation
They stood on the hot wharf where the current tugged
And the boats swung slanting.
Andreff, tipping his helmet, noted
The broad slow-swaying river's-back in the sun
And green without motion: the extravagant shade.

*

. . . And
A monkey's scream swung off like a pendulum
Between dark trunks of the jungle and heavy

Embellishments of growth which bright-winged birds
gripped
And secret, stinking pockets wherein stared
Malignant beads: the lidless eyes of spiders.
The slow express of a python, black and gold,
Thick with power oozed over branches.

*

From *The Destroyers*

ARCHIBALD FLEMING

Speech of the First Sentry

Now all things melt and shift in the moon's light.
The walls before you alter. The landscape
Alters. Familiar things
Take unfamiliar shape.
The building you knew at noon of such a height
Will shrink by dusk. The very street
That led you to your house begins to change,
And as you walk the thing within your mind
Takes form before the echo of your feet.
And there, behind the door you knew you locked yourself
Twist the key and find
A dead man in his winding sheet.

The knowledge you had at morning by the night
Will cope with nothing. The measured mile
Between two landmarks stretches and contracts.
Time no longer fixed
To the actuated shadow on a dial
Will break and waver like your image
In wind-blown water.
All laws have broken
According to some law you sense, but worse
Than none because you cannot understand,
Seeing it only as unappeasable curse
Making you stranger to your own hand.

All problems crossed–no sum
You learned at school will quite work out;
Nothing constant but the power
To prove upon the world your every doubt.
It is the moment of the whirlpool, moment
Of that abyss where all things stream.
O you who sleep tonight within this city!
Think now of order, for in what's to come
You'll learn how 'be' and 'seem'
May interchange along with 'plan' and 'chance'
And hear above your heads destruction dance
On the curved roof of the universe as a drum.

Tombstone with Cherubim

HORACE GREGORY

No notice in the papers,
only a voice over the telephone
Saying she was dead, casually,
remarkably definite.
Somebody whispered syphilis—
a sentimental lie.
Somebody spoke of her
(rococo) a Florentine olive tree
that should have twined (O unmistakably!)
around the person of a football-captain stock-broker
asleep
Upon Miami sands.
She shrieked at poverty.
divorced from silks, furs, and patented nickel-plated
limousines.
She loved relaxed security,
sleeping with men occasionally
as it were exotic dreams
and rich meaningless words
draping the tender portions of her body:
Hello, Marie!
you should have gone out like a row of mazda lamps
smashed with a crowbar.
Even this epitaph,
true enough for a beautiful girl

pacing with unforgettable ease
down Michigan Boulevard one April morning,
does not contain the facts.
                                                  The facts were these:
She died in Lesbian serenity
                                                      neither hot nor cold
until the chaste limbs stiffened.
                                                      Disconnect the telephone;
cut the wires.

Salvos for Randolph Bourne

HORACE GREGORY

O bitterness never spoken, the death mask etched in silver,
the dark limbs rolled in lead where the shallow grave conceals
despair: the image of a large head, forward, devouring
the collarbone. No general in brass over it and no
conquering angel kneels.

II

This was the end:
There were no firing squads
No City Hall Nathan Hale with a bronze cord at his throat
Speaking of lives and his country where a hundred million lives
rose, wavered, shattered like an invisible sea coiling
against a rock (no longer there) but sunken
into a shore line of weeds and sand.

Only a small room and a million words to be written before midnight
against poverty and idiot death like the gray face of Emerson
fading in New England winter twilight; the hard face vanishing

in snow, the passionately soft words issuing from the mouth—
O listen to the rock, the oracle no longer there!

III

To be the last American, an embryo coiled in a test tube,
To be a fixed and paralytic smile cocked upward to the clouds,
To see friends and enemies depart (around the corner)
Their sticks and smart fedoras bright in sunlight,
To be or not to be Hamlet, the Prince of Wales,
or last week's *New Republic;*
to be death delicately walking between chimney pots on Eighth Street,
possibly this is best to be
or not to be.

I Paint What I See

A Ballad of Artistic Integrity

E. B. WHITE

"What do you paint, when you paint a wall?"
  Said John D.'s grandson Nelson.
"Do you paint just anything there at all?
"Will there be any doves, or a tree in fall?
"Or a hunting scene, like an English hall?"

"I paint what I see," said Rivera.

"What are the colors you use when you paint?"
  Said John D.'s grandson Nelson.
"Do you use any red in the beard of a saint?
"If you do, is it terribly red, or faint?
"Do you use any blue? Is it Prussian?"

"I paint what I paint," said Rivera.

"Whose is that head that I see on my wall?"
  Said John D.'s grandson Nelson.
"Is it anyone's head whom we know, at all?
"A Rensselaer, or a Saltonstall?
"Is it Franklin D.? Is it Mordaunt Hall?
"Or is it the head of a Russian?"

"I paint what I think," said Rivera.

"I paint what I paint, I paint what I see,
"I paint what I think," said Rivera,

"And the thing that is dearest in life to me
"In a bourgeois hall is Integrity;
"However . . .
"I'll take out a couple of people drinkin'
"And put in a picture of Abraham Lincoln,
"I could even give you McCormick's reaper
"And still not make my art much cheaper.
"But the head of Lenin has got to stay
"Or my friends will give me the bird today
"The bird, the bird, forever."

"It's not good taste in a man like me,"
Said John D.'s grandson Nelson,
"To question an artist's integrity
"Or mention a practical thing like a fee,
"But I know what I like to a large degree
"Though art I hate to hamper;
"For twenty-one thousand conservative bucks
"You painted a radical. I say shucks,
"I never could rent the offices—
"The capitalistic offices.
"For this, as you know, is a public hall
"And people want doves, or a tree in fall,
"And though your art I dislike to hamper,
"I owe a *little* to God and Gramper,
"And after all,
"It's *my* wall . . ."

"We'll see if it is," said Rivera.

The Conspirators

FREDERIC PROKOSCH

And if the dead, and the dead
Of spirit now join, and in their horrifying ritual
Proceed till at last with oriental grace
End their concluding dance with the candles guttering,
The cymbals sobbing, the wind harassing the curtains,
The chill from the flood embracing the golden stairway.
The scent devoured and the bowls blown clean of
  incense:

Ah then, farewell, sweet northern music;
No longer the flight of the mind across the continents,
The dazzling flight of our words across the tempestuous
Black, or the firelit recital of a distant battle.

No. All that we loved is lost, if the intricate
Languor of recollected centuries
Descends in its terrible sweetness on our limbs.
No shot will echo; no fire; no agonizing
Cry will resound in the city's thickets: only,
The ivy falling gently across the bridges,
The larches piercing the roofs, the reclining steeples,
The cellars rich with the agony of the reptiles,
The contemplative worms, the victorious rodents,
And at last, the climax entrancingly serene,
The inconclusive note drowned on the ascendant:

Our lovely shapes in marble still shine through the
greenery,
Our exquisite silver bones still glide with the glaciers
That split our familiar hills, still fall with the avalanche
And weaving their vast wing's thunder over the Indies
The birds, the birds, sob for the time of man.

The Too-Late Born

ARCHIBALD MACLEISH

We too, we too, descending once again
The hills of our own land, we too have heard
Far off—Ah, que ce cor a longue haleine—
The horn of Roland in the passages of Spain,
The first, the second blast, the failing third,
And with the third turned back and climbed once more
The steep road southward, and heard faint the sound
Of swords, of horses, the disastrous war,
And crossed the dark defile at last, and found
At Roncevaux upon the darkening plain
The dead against the dead and on the silent ground
The silent slain—

From *Conquistador*

ARCHIBALD MAC LEISH

Bernál Díaz' Preface to His Book

'That which I have myself seen and the fighting' . . .

And I am an ignorant man: and this priest this
Gómara with the school-taught skip to his writing

The pompous Latin the appropriate feasts
The big names the imperial decorations
The beautiful battles and the brave deceased

The onward marches the wild Indian nations
The conquests sieges sorties wars campaigns
(And one eye always on the live relations)—

He with his famous history of New Spain—
This priest is a learned man: is not ignorant:
And I am poor: without gold: gainless:

My lands deserts in Guatemala: my fig-tree the
Spiked bush: my grapes thorns: my children
Half-grown: sons with beards: the big one

Breaking the small of his back in the brothel thills
And a girl to be married and all of them snarling at
  home
With the Indian look in their eyes like a cat killing:

And this Professor Francisco López de Gómara
Childless; not poor: and I am old: over eighty:
Stupid with sleepless nights: unused to the combing of

Words clean of the wool while the tale waits:
And he is a youthful man: a sound one: lightened with
Good sleep: skilled in the pen's plaiting—

I am an ignorant old sick man: blind with the
Shadow of death on my face and my hands to lead me:
And he not ignorant: not sick—
but I

Fought in those battles! These were my own deeds!
These names he writes of mouthing them out as a man would
Names in Herodotus—dead and their wars to read—

These were my friends: these dead my companions:
I: Bernál Díaz: called del Castíllo:
Called in the time of my first fights El Galán:

I here in the turn of the day in the feel of
Darkness to come now: moving my chair with the change:
Thinking too much these times how the doves would wheel at

Evening over my youth and the air's strangeness:
Thinking too much of my old town of Medina
And the Spanish dust and the smell of the true rain:

I: poor: blind in the sun: I have seen
With these eyes those battles: I saw Montezúma:
I saw the armies of Mexico marching the leaning

Wind in their garments: the painted faces: the plumes
Blown on the light air: I saw that city:
I walked at night on those stones: in the shadowy rooms

I have heard the chink of my heel and the bats twit-
  tering:
I: poor as I am: I was young in that country:
These words were my life: these letters written

Cold on the page with the split ink and the shunt of the
Stubborn thumb: these marks at my fingers:
These are the shape of my own life . . .

and I hunted the
Unknown birds in the west with their beautiful wings!

Old men should die with their time's span:
The sad thing is not death: the sad thing

Is the life's loss out of earth when the living vanish:
All that was good in the throat: the hard going:
The marching singing in sunshine: the showery land:

The quick loves: the sleep: the waking: the blowing of
Winds over us: all this that we knew:
All this goes out at the end as the flowing of

Water carries the leaves down: and the few—
Three or four there are of us still that remember it—
Perish: and that time's stopt like a stale tune:

And the bright young masters with their bitter treble
Understanding it all like an old game!
And the pucker of art on their lips like the pip of a
lemon!—

'The tedious veteran jealous of his fame!'
What is my fame or the fame of these my companions?
Their tombs are the bellies of Indians: theirs are the
shameful

Graves in the wild earth: in the Godless sand:
None know the place of their bones: as for mine
Strangers will dig my grave in a stony land:

Even my sons have the strangeness of dark kind in them:
Indian dogs will bark at dusk by my sepulchre:
What is my fame! But those days: the shine of the

Sun in that time: the wind then: the step
Of the moon over those leaf-fallen nights: the sleet in
the
Dry grass: the smell of the dust where we slept—

These things were real: these suns had heat in them:
This was brine in the mouth: bitterest foam:
Earth: water to drink: bread to be eaten—

Not the sound of a word like the writing of Gómara:
Not a past time: a year: the name of a
Battle lost—'and the Emperor Charles came home

'That year: and that was the year the same
'They fought in Flanders and the Duke was hung—'
The dates of empire: the dry skull of fame!

No but our lives: the days of our lives: we were young
then:
The strong sun was standing in deep trees:
We drank at the springs: the thongs of our swords
unslung to it:

We saw that city on the inland sea:
Towers between: and the green-crowned Montezúma
Walking the gardens of shade: and the staggering bees:

And the girls bearing the woven baskets of bloom on
their
Black hair: their breasts alive: and the hunters
Shouldering dangling herons with their ruffled plumes:

We were the first that found that famous country:
We marched by a king's name: we crossed the sierras:
Unknown hardships we suffered: hunger:

Death by the stone knife: thirst: we fared by the
Bitter streams: we came at last to that water:
Towers were steep upon the fluttering air:

We were the lords of it all . . .
                                        Now time has taught us:
Death has mastered us most: sorrow and pain
Sickness and evil days are our lives' lot:

Now even the time of our youth has been taken:
Now are our deeds words: our lives chronicles:
Afterwards none will think of the night rain. . . .

How shall a man edure the will of God and the
Days and the silence!
                              In the world before us
Neither in Cuba nor the isles beyond–

Not Fonséca himself the sagging whore–
Not the Council the Audience even the Indians–
Knew of a land to the west: they skirted the Floridas:

They ran the islands on the bare-pole winds:
They touched the Old Main and the midland shores:
They saw the sun go down at the gulf's beginning:

None had sailed to the west and returned till Córdova:
I went in that ship: Alvarez handled her:
Trusting to luck: keeping the evening before him:

Sighting after the third week land
And no report of a land there in that ocean:
The Indians clean: wearing the delicate bands:

Cape Catoche we called it: 'conës catoche'—
So they cried to us over the sea flood:
Many idols they had for their devotion

Some of women: some coupled in sodomy
So we sailed on: we came to Campéchë:
There by the sweet pool they kindled the wood-fire:

Words they were saying like 'Castilán' in their speech:
They warned us by signs to be gone when the logs
  charred:
So we turned from them down to the smooth beaches:

The boats followed us close in: we departed:
Afterwards there was a *nortë* with fine haze:
We stood for Potonchán through the boil of the narrows:

There they attacked us crossing the green of the maize
  fields:
Me they struck thrice and they killed fifty
And all were hurt and two taken crazy with

Much pain and it blew and the dust lifted
And the thirst cracked the tongues in our mouths and
  before us the
Sea-corrupted pools where the river drifts:

And we turned back and the wind drove us to Florida:
There in the scooped sand in the withered bed—
There by the sea they encountered us threatening war:

So we returned to the islands half dead:
And Córdova did die: and we wrote to Velásquez—
Diégo the Governor—writing it out: and we said—

'Excellence: there are lands in the west: the pass is
'Clean sailing: the scuts of the men are covered:
'The houses are masonry: gold they have: baskets

'Painted with herbs: the women are chaste in love'—
Much else of the kind I cannot remember:
And Velásquez took the credit for this discovery:

And all we had was our wounds: and enough of them:
And Fonséca Bishop of Búrgos (for so he was called)
President of the Council: he wrote to the Emperor

Telling the wonderful news in a mule's volley
And not a word of our deeds or our pains or our battles:
And Charles gone: and Joanna the poor queen stalled

In Tordesíllas shaking the peas in a rattle:
And Barbarossa licking his chin in Algiers:
And trouble enough in Spain with all that

And the Cardinal dying and Sicily over the ears—
Trouble enough without new lands to be conquered
 and
Naked Indians taken and wild sheep sheared:

But as for us that returned from that westward country—
We could not lie in our towns for the sound of the sea:
We could not rest at all in our thoughts: we were young then:

We looked to the west: we remembered the foreign trees
Borne out on the tide from the unknown rivers
And the clouds like hills in the air our eyes had seen:

And Grijálva sailed next and we that were living—
We that had gear to our flesh and the gold to find
And an old pike in the stall with the haft to it slivered—

We signed on and we sailed by the first tide:
And we fought at Potonchán that voyage: I remember
The locusts covered the earth like a false shine to it:

They flew with a shrill sound like the arrow stem:
Often we took the whir of the darts for the locusts:
Often we left our shields from our mouths as they came:

I remember our fighting was much marred by the locusts:
And that voyage we came to the river Tabasco:
We saw the nets as we came in and the smoke of the

Sea over the bar: and we filled the casks there:
There first we heard of the farther land—
'Colua' they said 'Méjico'—we that were asking the

Gold there on that shore on the evening sand—
'Colua' they said: pointing on toward the sunset:
They made a sign on the air with their solemn hands:

Afterward: north: on the sea: and the ships running
We saw the steep snow mountain on the sky:
We stared as dream-awakened men in wonder:

And that voyage it was we came to the Island:
Well I remember the shore and the sound of that place
And the smoke smell on the dunes and the wind dying:

Well I remember the walls and the rusty taste of the
New-spilled blood in the air: many among us
Seeing the priests with their small and arrogant faces:

Seeing the dead boys' breasts and the idols hung with
the
Dried shells of the hearts like the husks of cicadas
And their human eyeballs and their painted tongues

Cried out to the Holy Mother of God for it:
And some that stood there bore themselves the stone:
And some were eaten of wild beasts of their bodies:

And none of us all but had his heart foreknown the
Evil to come would have turned from the land then:
But the lives of men are covered and not shown—

Only late to the old at their time's ending
The land shows backward and the way is there:
And the next day we sailed and the sea was against us

And our bread was dirty with weevils and grown scarce
and the
Rains began and the beans stank in the ovens
And we soldiers were thoroughly tired of sea-faring:

So we returned from that voyage with God's love:
And they talked about nothing else in the whole of
Cuba:
And gentlemen sold their farms to go on discoveries:

And we that had fought in the marshes with no food—
We sat by the palms in the square in the green gloaming
With the delicate girls on our knees and the night to
lose:

We that had fought in those lands . . .
and the eloquent Gómara:
The quilled professors: the taught tongues of fame:
What have they written of us: the poor soldiers:

We that were wounded often for no pay:
We that died and were dumped cold in the bread sacks:
Bellies up: the birds at us: floating for days

And none remembering which it was that was dead there
Whether of Búrgos or Yúste or Villalár:
Where have they written our names? What have they said of us?

They call the towns for the kings that bear no scars:
They keep the names of the great for time to stare at—
The bishops rich-men generals cocks-at-arms:

Those with the glaze in their eyes and the fine bearing:
The born leaders of men: the resonant voices:
They give them the lands for their tombs: they call it America!

(And who has heard of Vespucci in this soil
Or down by the lee of the coast or toward the Havana?)
And we that fought here: that with heavy toil

Earthed up the powerful cities of this land—
What are we? When will our fame come?
An old man in a hill town
a handful of

Dust under the dry grass at Otúmba

Unknown names
hands vanished
faces

Many gone from the day
                                        unspeakable numbers
Lives forgotten
                              deeds honored in strangers
'That which I have myself seen and the fighting' . . .

Invocation to the Social Muse

ARCHIBALD MACLEISH

Señora it is true the Greeks are dead:

It is true also that we here are Americans:
That we use the machines: that a sight of the god is
  unusual:
That more people have more thoughts: that there are

Progress and science and tractors and revolutions and
Marx and the wars more antiseptic and murderous
And music in every home: there is also Hoover:

Does the lady suggest we should write it out in The
  Word?
Does Madame recall our responsibilities? We are
Whores Fraulein: poets Fraulein are persons of

Known vocation following troops: they must sleep with
Stragglers from either prince and of both views:
The rules permit them to further the business of neither:

It is also strictly forbidden to mix in maneuvers:
Those that infringe are inflated with praise on the
  plazas—
Their bones are resultantly afterwards found under
  newspapers:

Preferring life with the sons to death with the fathers
We also doubt on the record whether the sons
Will still be shouting around with the same huzzas—

For we hope Lady to live to lie with the youngest:
There are only a handful of things a man likes
Generation to generation hungry or

Well fed: the earth's one: life's
One: Mister Morgan is not one:

There is nothing worse for our trade than to be in style:

He that goes naked goes farther at last than another:
Wrap the bard in a flag or a school and they'll jimmy his
Door down and be thick in his bed—for a month:

(Who recalls the address now of the Imagists?)
But the naked man has always his own nakedness:
People remember forever his live limbs:

They may drive him out of the camps but one will take
  him:
They may stop his tongue on his teeth with a rope's
  argument—
He will lie in a house and be warm when they are
  shaking:

Besides Tovarishch how to embrace an army?
How to take to one's chamber a million souls?
How to conceive in the name of a column of marchers?

The things of the poet are done to a man alone
As the things of love are done—or of death when he
hears the
Step withdraw on the stair and the clock tick only:

Neither his class nor his kind nor his trade may come
near him
There where he lies on his left arm and will die:
Nor his class nor his kind nor his trade when the blood
is jeering

And his knee's in the soft of the bed where his love lies:

I remind you Barinya the life of the poet is hard—
A hardy life with a boot as quick as a fiver:

Is it just to demand of us also to bear arms?

Burying Ground by the Ties

ARCHIBALD MAC LEISH

Ayee! Ai! This is heavy earth on our shoulders:
There were none of us born to be buried in this earth:
Niggers we were Portuguese Magyars Polacks:

We were born to another look of the sky certainly:
Now we lie here in the river pastures:
We lie in the mowings under the thick turf:

We hear the earth and the all-day rasp of the grasshoppers:
It was we laid the steel on this land from ocean to
ocean:
It was we (if you know) put the U. P. through the
passes

Bringing her down into Laramie full load
Eighteen mile on the granite anticlinal
Forty-three foot to the mile and the grade holding:

It was we did it: hunkies of our kind:
It was we dug the caved-in holes for the cold water:
It was we built the gully spurs and the freight sidings:

Who would do it but we and the Irishmen bossing us?
It was all foreign-born men there were in this country:
It was Scotsmen Englishmen Chinese Squareheads
Austrians . . .

Ayee! but there's weight to the earth under it:
Not for this did we come out—to be lying here
Nameless under the ties in the clay cuts:

There's nothing good in the world but the rich will
 buy it:
Everything sticks to the grease of a gold note—
Even a continent—even a new sky!

Do not pity us much for the strange grass over us:
We laid the steel to the stone stock of these mountains:
The place of our graves is marked by the telegraph
 poles!

It was not to lie in the bottoms we came out
And the trains going over us here in the dry hollows . . .

Oil Painting of the Artist As the Artist

ARCHIBALD MAC LEISH

The plump Mr. Pl'f is washing his hands of America:
The plump Mr. Pl'f is in ochre with such hair:

America is in blue-black-grey-green-sandcolor:
America is a continent—many lands:

The plump Mr. Pl'f is washing his hands of America:
He is pictured at Pau on the *place* and his eyes glaring:

He thinks of himself as an exile from all this:
As an émigré from his own time into history—

(History being an empty house without owners
A practical man may get in by the privy stones—

The dead are excellent hosts: they have no objections—
And once in he can nail the knob on the next one

Living the life of a classic in bad air with
Himself for the Past and his face in the glass for Posterity)

The Cinquecento is nothing at all like Nome
Or Natchez or Wounded Knee or the Shenandoah:

Your vulgarity Tennessee: your violence Texas:
The rocks under your fields Ohio Connecticut:

Your clay Missouri your clay: you have driven him out:
You have shadowed his life Appalachians purple mountains:

There is much too much of your flowing Mississippi:
He prefers a tidier stream with a terrace for trippers and

Cypresses mentioned in Horace or Henry James:
He prefers a country where everything carries the name of a

Countess or real king or an actual palace or
Something in Prose and the stock prices all in Italian:

There is more shade for an artist under a fig
Than under the whole damn range (he finds) of the Big Horns

Pole Star for This Year

ARCHIBALD MAC LEISH

Where the wheel of light is turned:
Where the axle of the night is
Turned: is motionless: where holds
And has held ancient sureness always:

Where of faring men the eyes
At oar bench at the rising bow
Have seen—torn shrouds between—the Wain
And that star's changelessness: not changing:

There upon that intent star:
Trust of wandering men: of truth
The most reminding witness: we
Fix our eyes also: waylost: the wanderers:

We too turn now to that star:
We too in whose trustless hearts
All truth alters and the lights
Of earth are out now turn to that star:

Liberty of man and mind
That once was mind's necessity
And made the West blaze up has burned
To bloody embers and the lamp's out:

Hope that was a noble flame
Has fanned to violence and feeds
On cities and the flesh of men
And chokes where unclean smoke defiles it:

Even the small spark of pride
That taught the tyrant once is dark
Where gunfire rules the starving street
And justice cheats the dead of honor:

Liberty and pride and hope
And every guide-mark of the mind
That led our blindness once has vanished.
This star will not. Love's star will not.

Love that has beheld the face
A man has with a man's eyes in it
Bloody from the slugger's blows
Or heard the cold child cry for hunger—

Love that listens where the good:
The virtuous: the men of faith:
Proclaim the paradise on earth
And murder starve and burn to make it—

Love that cannot either sleep
Or keep rich music in the ear
Or lose itself for the wild beat
The anger in the blood makes raging—

Love that hardens into hate—
Love like hatred and as bright—
Love is that one waking light
That leads now when all others darken.

PART FOUR

These are the live,
Not silhouettes or dead men.
That dull murmur is their tread on the street.
Those brass quavers are their shouts.
Here is the wind blowing through the crowded square.
Here is the violence and secret change.
And these are figures of life beneath the sea.
These are the lovely women
And the exhilarations that die.
Here is a stone lying on the sidewalk
In the shadow of the wall.
Hey? What saith the noble poet now,
Drawing his hand across his brow?
Claude, is the divine afflatus upon you?
Hey? Hey Claude?
Here are a million taxi drivers, social prophets,
The costume for an attitude,
A back-stage shriek,
The heat and speed of the earth.
Here is a statue of Burns.
There is the modern moon.
That song is the latest dance.
Hey? Of what doth the noble poet brood
In a tragic mood?

—Kenneth Fearing

Song of Songs

WILFRED OWEN

Sing me at morn but only with your laugh;
Even as Spring that laugheth into leaf;
Even as Love that laugheth after Life.

Sing me but only with your speech all day,
As voluble leaflets do; let viols die;
The least word of your lips is melody!

Sing me at eve but only with your sigh!
Like lifting seas it solaceth; breathe so,
Slowly and low, the sense that no songs say.

Sing me at midnight with your murmurous heart!
Let youth's immortal-moaning chords be heard
Throbbing through you, and sobbing, unsubdued.

The Show

WILFRED OWEN

We have fallen in the dreams the ever-living
Breathe on the tarnished mirror of the world,
And then smooth out with ivory hands and sigh
W. B. Yeats

My soul looked down from a vague height with Death,
As unremembering how I rose or why,
And saw a sad land, weak with sweats of dearth,
Gray, cratered like the moon with hollow woe,
And pitted with great pocks and scabs of plagues.

Across its beard, that horror of harsh wire,
There moved thin caterpillars, slowly uncoiled.
It seemed they pushed themselves to be as plugs
Of ditches, where they writhed and shrivelled, killed.

By them had slimy paths been trailed and scraped
Round myriad warts that might be little hills.

From gloom's last dregs these long-strung creatures crept,
And vanished out of dawn down hidden holes.

(And smell came up from those foul openings
As out of mouths, or deep wounds deepening.)

On dithering feet upgathered, more and more,
Brown strings, towards strings of gray, with bristling
spines,
All migrants from green fields, intent on mire.

Those that were gray, of more abundant spawns,
Ramped on the rest and ate them and were eaten.

I saw their bitten backs curve, loop, and straighten,
I watched those agonies curl, lift, and flatten.

Whereat, in terror what that sight might mean,
I reeled and shivered earthward like a feather.

And Death fell with me, like a deepening moan.
And He, picking a manner of worm, which half had hid
Its bruises in the earth, but crawled no further,
Showed me its feet, the feet of many men,
And the fresh-severed head of it, my head.

Arms and the Boy

WILFRED OWEN

Let the boy try along this bayonet-blade
How cold steel is, and keen with hunger of blood;
Blue with all malice, like a madman's flash;
And thinly drawn with famishing for flesh.

Lend him to stroke these blind, blunt bullet-heads
Which long to nuzzle in the hearts of lads,
Or give him cartridges of fine zinc teeth,
Sharp with the sharpness of grief and death.

For his teeth seem for laughing round an apple.
There lurk no claws behind his fingers supple;
And god will grow no talons at his heels,
Nor antlers through the thickness of his curls.

Strange Meeting

WILFRED OWEN

It seemed that out of battle I escaped
Down some profound dull tunnel, long since scooped
Through granites which titanic wars had groined.
Yet also there encumbered sleepers groaned,
Too fast in thought or death to be bestirred.
Then, as I probed them, one sprang up, and stared
With piteous recognition in fixed eyes,
Lifting distressful hands as if to bless.
And by his smile, I knew that sullen hall,
By his dead smile I knew we stood in Hell.
With a thousand pains that vision's face was grained;
Yet no blood reached there from the upper ground,
And no guns thumped, or down the flues made moan.
"Strange friend," I said, "here is no cause to mourn."
"None," said the other, "save the undone years,
The hopelessness. Whatever hope is yours,
Was my life also; I went hunting wild
After the wildest beauty in the world,
Which lies not calm in eyes, or braided hair,
But mocks the steady running of the hour,
And if it grieves, grieves richlier than here.
For by my glee might many men have laughed,
And of my weeping something had been left,
Which must die now. I mean the truth untold,
The pity of war, the pity war distilled.

Now men will go content with what we spoiled.
Or discontent, boil bloody, and be spilled.
They will be swift with swiftness of the tigress,
None will break ranks, though nations trek from progress.
Courage was mine, and I had mystery,
Wisdom was mine and I had mastery;
To miss the march of this retreating world
Into vain citadels that are not walled.
Then, when much blood had clogged their chariot-
wheels
I would go up and wash them from sweet wells,
Even with truths that lie too deep for taint.
I would have poured my spirit without stint
But not through wounds; not on the cess of war.
Foreheads of men have bled where no wounds were.
I am the enemy you killed, my friend.
I knew you in this dark; for so you frowned
Yesterday through me as you jabbed and killed.
I parried; but my hands were loath and cold.
Let us sleep now. . . ."

Greater Love

WILFRED OWEN

Red lips are not so red
  As the stained stones kissed by the English dead.
Kindness of wooed and wooer
Seems shame to their love pure.
O Love, your eyes lose lure
  When I behold eyes blinded in my stead!

Your slender attitude
  Trembles not exquisite like limbs knife-skewed,
Rolling and rolling there
Where God seems not to care;
Till the fierce Love they bear
  Cramps them in death's extreme decrepitude.

Your voice sings not so soft,—
  Though even as wind murmuring through raftered
    loft,—
Your dear voice is not dear,
Gentle, and evening clear,
As theirs whom none now hear,
  Now earth has stopped their piteous mouths that
    coughed.

Heart, you were never hot,
  Nor large, nor full like hearts made great with shot;

And though your hand be pale,
Paler are all which trail
Your cross through flame and hail:
  Weep, you may weep, for you may touch them not.

Disabled

WILFRED OWEN

He sat in a wheeled chair, waiting for dark,
And shivered in his ghastly suit of grey,
Legless, sewn short at elbow. Through the park
Voices of boys rang saddening like a hymn,
Voices of play and pleasures after day
Till gathering sleep had mothered them from him.

. . . . .

About this time Town used to swing so gay
When glow-lamps budded in the light blue trees,
And girls glanced lovelier as the air grew dim,—
In the old times, before he threw away his knees.
Now he will never feel again how slim
Girls' waists are, or how warm their subtle hands;
All of them touch him like some queer disease.

. . . . .

There was an artist silly for his face,
For it was younger than his youth, last year.
Now, he is old; his back will never brace;
He's lost his colour very far from here,
Poured it down shell-holes till the veins ran dry,
And half his lifetime lapsed in the hot race,
And leap of purple spurted from his thigh.

. . . . .

One time he liked a blood-smear down his leg,
After the matches, carried shoulder-high.
It was after football, when he'd drunk a peg,
He thought he'd better join.—He wonders why.
Someone had said he'd look a god in kilts,
That's why; and may be, too, to please his Meg;
Aye, that was it, to please the giddy jilts
He asked to join. He didn't have to beg;
Smiling they wrote his lie; aged nineteen years.
Germans he scarcely thought of; all their guilt,
And Austria's did not move him. And no fears
Of Fear came yet. He thought of jewelled hilts
For daggers in plaid socks; of smart salutes;
And care of arms; and leave; and pay arrears;
Esprit de corps; and hints for young recruits.
And soon he was drafted out with drums and cheers.

. . . . .

Some cheered him home, but not as crowds cheer Goal.
Only a solemn man who brought him fruits,
Thanked him; and then inquired about his soul.

. . . . .

Now he will spend a few sick years in Institutes,
And do what things the rules consider wise,
And take whatever pity they may dole.
To-night he noticed how the women's eyes
Passed from him to the strong men that were whole.
How cold and late it is! Why don't they come
And put him into bed? Why don't they come?

To My Friend

(With an Identity Disc)

WILFRED OWEN

If ever I had dreamed of my dead name
  High in the heart of London, unsurpassed
By Time for ever, and the Fugitive, Fame,
  There seeking a long sanctuary at last,—

Or if I onetime hoped to hide its shame,
  —Shame of success, and sorrow of defeats,—
Under those holy cypresses, the same
  That shade always the quiet place of Keats,

Now rather thank I God there is no risk
  Of gravers scoring it with florid screed.
Let my inscription be this soldier's disc. . . .
  Wear it, sweet friend, inscribe no date nor deed.
But may thy heart-beat kiss it, night and day,
Until the name grow blurred and fade away.

1918

Dirge

KENNETH FEARING

1-2-3 was the number he played but today the number came 3-2-1;
bought his Carbide at 30 and it went to 29; had the favorite at Bowie but the track was slow—

O, executive type, would you like to drive a floating power, knee-action, silk-upholstered six? Wed a Hollywood star? Shoot the course in 58? Draw to the ace, king, jack?
O, fellow with a will who won't take no, watch out for three cigarettes on the same, single match; O, democratic voter born in August under Mars, beware of liquidated rails—

Denouement to denouement, he took a personal pride in the certain, certain way he lived his own, private life,
but nevertheless, they shut off his gas; nevertheless, the bank foreclosed; nevertheless, the landlord called; nevertheless, the radio broke,

And twelve o'clock arrived just once too often,
just the same he wore one grey tweed suit, bought one straw hat, drank one straight Scotch, walked one short step, took one long look, drew one deep breath,
just one too many,

And wow he died as wow he lived,
going whop to the office and blooie home to sleep and biff got married and bam had children and oof got fired,
zowie did he live and zowie did he die,

With who the hell are you at the corner of his casket, and where the hell we going on the right hand silver knob, and who the hell cares walking second from the end with an American Beauty wreath from why the hell not,

Very much missed by the circulation staff of the New York Evening Post; deeply, deeply mourned by the B.M.T.,

Wham, Mr. Roosevelt; pow, Sears Roebuck; awk, big dipper; bop, summer rain;
bong, Mr., bong, Mr., bong, Mr., bong.

Museums

LOUIS MACNEICE

Museums offer us, running from among the 'buses,
A centrally heated refuge, parquet floors and sarcophaguses,
Into whose tall fake porches we hurry without a sound
Like a beetle under a brick that lies, useless on the ground.
Warmed and cajoled by the silence, the cowed cipher revives,
Mirrors himself in the cases of pots, paces himself by marble lives,
Makes believe it was he that was the glory that was Rome,
Soft on his cheek the nimbus of other people's martyrdom,
And then returns to the street, his mind an arena where sprawls
Any number of consumptive Keatses and dying Gauls.

Their Last Will and Testament

LOUIS MACNEICE

(With W. H. Auden)

We, Wystan Hugh Auden and Louis MacNeice,
Brought up to speak and write the English tongue
Being led in the eighteenth year of the Western Peace

To the duck-shaped mountainous island with the Danish King,
At Melgraseyri in Isafjördardjup
Under the eaves of a glacier, considering

The autumns, personal and public, which already creep
Through city-crowded Europe, and those in want
Who soon must look up at the winter sky and weep.

Do set down this, our will and testament:
Believing man responsible for what he does,
Sole author of his terror and his content.

*

We leave to Stanley Baldwin, our beloved P.M.,
The false front of Lincoln Cathedral, and a school
Of Empire poets. As for his Cabinet, to them

We leave their National character and strength of will.
To Winston Churchill Ballinrobe's dry harbour
And Randolph, un bel pezzo, in a codicil.

To Sir Maurice Hankey for his secretarial labour
The Vicar of Bray's discretion; and to Lord Lloyd
We leave a flag-day and a cavalry sabre.

To Vickers the Gran Chaco (for agents must be paid),
The Balkan Conscience and the sleepless night we think
The inevitable diseases of their dangerous trade.

*

Item, to I. A. Richards who like a mouse
Nibbles linguistics with the cerebral tooth
We leave a quiet evening in a boarding-house

Where he may study the facts of birth and death
In their inexplicable oddity
And put a shilling in the slot for brains and breath.

And Julian Huxley we leave an ant, a bee,
An axolotl and Aldous; item, to Bert-
rand Russell we leave belief in God (D.V.)

Item, we leave a bottle of invalid port
To Lady Astor; item, the Parthenon
On the Calton Hill to Basil de Selincourt.

Item, we leave the phases of the moon
To Mr. Yeats to rock his bardic sleep;
And to Dr. Cyril Norwood a new spittoon;

And Tubby Clayton can have some gingerpop;
And General O'Duffy can take the Harp That Once
Started and somehow was never able to stop.

We leave a mens sana qui mal y pense
To the Public Schools of England, plus Ian Hay
That the sons of gents may have La Plus Bonne Chance.

*

And to Sir Oswald (please forgive the stench
Which taints our parchment from that purulent name)
We leave a rather unpleasant word in French.

*

. . . .

As for the parts of our bodies in this will

We allot them here as follows: to the Home
For Lost Dogs and Cats our livers and lights,
And our behinds to the Birmingham Hippodrome.

And our four eyes which cannot see for nuts
We leave to all big-game hunters and to all
Apprentices to murder at the butts;

Our feet to hikers when their own feet fail;
To all escapists our Islands of Langerhans;
And to Imperial Chemicals a pail

Of what in us would otherwise join the drains:
The Watch Committee can have our noses and
The British Association can have our brains:

Item, our ears, apt for the slightest sound,
We leave those Statesmen who happen to be debarred
From hearing how the wheels of State run round. . . .

*

To all the dictators who look so bold and fresh
The midnight hours, the soft wind from the sweeping
  wing
Of madness, and the intolerable tightening of the mesh

Of history. We leave their marvellous native tongue
To Englishmen, and for our intelligent island pray
That to her virtuous beauties by all poets sung

She add at last an honest foreign policy.
For her oppressed, injured, insulted, and weak
The logic and the passion proper for victory.

We leave our age the quite considerable spark
Of private love and goodness which never leaves
An age, however awful, in the utter dark.

We leave the unconceived and unborn lives
A closer approximation to real happiness
Than has been reached by us, our neighbours or their
  wives.

To those who by office or from inclination use
Authority, a knowledge of their own misdeed
And all the hate that coercion must produce.

For the lost who from self-hatred cannot hide,
Such temporary refuge or engines of escape
From pain as Chance and Mercy can provide

And to the good who know how wide the gulf, how deep
Between Ideal and Real, who being good have felt
The final temptation to withdraw, sit down and weep,

We pray the power to take upon themselves the guilt
Of human action, though still as ready to confess
The imperfection of what can and must be built,
The wish and power to act, forgive, and bless.

Tempt Me No More; for I

C. DAY LEWIS

Tempt me no more; for I
Have known the lightning's hour,
The poet's inward pride,
The certainty of power.

Bayonets are closing round.
I shrink; yet I must wring
A living from despair
And out of steel a song.

Though song, though breath be short,
I'll share not the disgrace
Of those that ran away
Or never left the base.

Comrades, my tongue can speak
No comfortable words,
Calls to a forlorn hope,
Gives work and not rewards.

Oh keep the sickle sharp
And follow still the plough:
Others may reap, though some
See not the winter through.

Father, who endest all,
Pity our broken sleep;
For we lie down with tears
And waken but to weep.

And if our blood alone
Will melt this iron earth,
Take it. It is well spent
Easing a saviour's birth.

Consider These, for We Have Condemned Them

C. DAY LEWIS

Consider these, for we have condemned them;
Leaders to no sure land, guides their bearings lost
Or in league with robbers have reversed the signposts,
Disrespectful to ancestors, irresponsible to heirs.
Born barren, a freak growth, root in rubble,
Fruitlessly blossoming, whose foliage suffocates,
Their sap is sluggish, they reject the sun.

The man with his tongue in his cheek, the woman
With her heart in the wrong place, unhandsome, unwholesome;
Have exposed the new-born to worse than weather,
Exiled the honest and sacked the seer.
These drowned the farms to form a pleasure-lake,
In time of drought they drain the reservoir
Through private pipes for baths and sprinklers.

Getters not begetters; gainers not beginners;
Whiners, no winners; no triers, betrayers;
Who steer by no star, whose moon means nothing.
Daily denying, unable to dig:
At bay in villas from blood relations,
Counters of spoons and content with cushions
They pray for peace, they hand down disaster.

They that take the bribe shall perish by the bribe,
Drying of dry rot, ending in asylums,
A curse to children, a charge on the state.
But still their fears and frenzies infect us;
Drug nor isolation will cure this cancer:
It is now or never, the hour of the knife,
The break with the past, the major operation.

Rapid Transit

JAMES AGEE

Squealing under city stone
  The millions on the millions run,
Every one a life alone,
  Every one a soul undone:

There all the poisons of the heart
  Branch and abound like whirling brooks
And there through every useless art
  Like spoiled meats on a butcher's hooks

Pour forth upon their frightful kind
  The faces of each ruined child:
The wrecked demeanors of the mind
  That now is tamed, and once was wild.

Millions Are Learning How

JAMES AGEE

From now on kill America out of your mind.
America is dead these hundred years.
You've better work to do, and things to find:
  Waste neither time nor tears.

See, rather, all the millions and all the land
Mutually shapen as a child of love.
As individual as a hand
  And to be thought highly of.

The wrinkling mountains stay: the master stream
Still soils the Gulf a hundred amber miles:
A people as a creature in a dream
  Not yet awakened, smiles.

Those poisons which were low along the air
Like mists, like mists are lifting. Even now,
Thousands are breathing health in, here and there:
  Millions are learning how.

Standard Forgings Plant

WILLIAM STEPHENS

All day, all night, we hear, we feel
  the dull, continual thud
of drop-forge hammers poundings steel
to axle-shape and shafted wheel,
  to coupling, tie-plate, bolt and stud.
Through long, low blocks of dirtv red
  faded by rain and sun
Those hammers fall in shed past shed
that under foot and over head
  move with the plunge of ton on ton.
Their impact rocks the solid ground,
  sand, shale, clay, granite-stone:
in street and house for blocks around
the heavy shock, the hollow sound
  shake walls, floors, windows, brain and bone.

The Eyes Have It

WILLIAM STEPHENS

Mister chairman and ladies and gentlemen
and brothers and sisters and fellow citizens:
what is our country now, that we should eye
and not see red, the fellow in the red necktie,
daughter's dangerous boyfriend at the door
who talks ignorance about wages and against war
while our true sons boot footballs over goals?

Haven't we cast our ballots from the polls,
sold goods and offices? I put it to you, I
put it to you. . . . The ayes have it: the eyes,
mister chairman, have that intelligent look that comes
at times like this; and not from studying over books,
but from the sound when bugles echo drums,
when dads see red and sons put up their dukes!

(The eyes have a concerted look that sums
up something: not that drunken bum's, old pal
the cop dragged up out of the ship canal,
no longer thirsty . . . nor that tired girl's
who rouged her lips, who frizzed her hair in curls,
swaying her hips, and hummed, and muttered "Dearie"
for any man to hear who would pay to look.)

The thing demands an answer: Shall our daughters
be friends with agitators, hold their hands
and even cohabit with them? My thoughts falter!
The idea makes my inside sick and should make yours.
I don't know any more how the home endures
when children mock their folks with smart replies
and wisecracks that a man can't understand!

The ayes have it, mister chairman: the ayes,
the eyes have that determined look that tells
a man's home town is no place for radicals
and college pacifists who disturb the peace!
Haven't we signed this country up on lease,
on business lines? You tell me, now: you say
if any eyes see better than ours today!

(The eyes have a deserted look that stares
not seeing them, at the disused room, the chairs
where daughter placed them, and the empty bed. . . .
What if they should see that seamstress, lying dead
on the embalming table, who became weary
straining to sew shirt-buttons, row on row,
in factories, where the eyes see what they know?)

Three Rhymes from *Hard Lines*

OGDEN NASH

1. Lines in Dispraise of Dispraise

I hereby bequeath to the Bide-a-Wee Home all people
who have statistics to prove that a human
Is nothing but a combination of iron and water and
potash and albumen.
That may very well be the truth
But it's just like saying that a cocktail is nothing
but ice and gin and vermouth.
People who go around analyzing
Are indeed very tanalizing.
They always want to get at the bottom
Of everything from spring to ottom.
They can't just look at a Rembrandt or a Bartolozzi
And say, Boy! that's pretty hozzi-tozzi!
No, they have to break it up into its component parts
And reconstruct it with blueprints and charts.
My idea is that while after looking around me and
even at me
I may not be proud of being a human
I object to having attention called to my iron and water
and potash and albumen.
In the first place, it's undignified,
And in the second place, nothing by it is signified.
Because it isn't potash etcetera that makes people

Republicans or Democrats or Ghibellines or Guelphs,
It's the natural perversity of the people themselfs.
No, no, you old analysts, away with the whole kit and
kaboodle of you.
I wouldn't even make mincemeat to give to a poodle of
you.

2. Song of the Open Road

I think that I shall never see
A billboard lovely as a tree.
Perhaps, unless the billboards fall,
I'll never see a tree at all.

3. Autres Bêtes, Autres Moeurs

(i)

The fish, when he's exposed to air
Can show no trace of savoir faire
But in the sea regains his balance
And exploits all his manly talents;
The chastest of the vertebrates,
He never even sees his mates,
But when they've finished, he appears
And O.K.'s all their bright ideas.

(ii)

The turtle lives 'twixt plated decks
Which practically conceal its sex.
I think it clever of the turtle
In such a fix to be so fertile.

The Express

STEPHEN SPENDER

After the first powerful plain manifesto
The black statement of pistons, without more fuss
But gliding like a queen, she leaves the station.
Without bowing and with restrained unconcern
She passes the houses which humbly crowd outside,
The gasworks and at last the heavy page
Of death, printed by gravestones in the cemetery.
Beyond the town there lies the open country
Where, gathering speed, she acquires mystery,
The luminous self-possession of ships on ocean.
It is now she begins to sing—at first quite low
Then loud, and at last with a jazzy madness—
The song of her whistle screaming at curves,
Of deafening tunnels, brakes, innumerable bolts.
And always light, aerial, underneath
Goes the elate metre of her wheels.
Steaming through metal landscape on her lines
She plunges new eras of wild happiness
Where speed throws up strange shapes, broad curves
And parallels clean like the steel of guns.
At last, further than Edinburgh or Rome,
Beyond the crest of the world she reaches night
Where only a low streamline brightness

Of phosphorus on the tossing hills is white.
Ah, like a comet through flame she moves entranced
Wrapt in her music no bird song, no, nor bough
Breaking with honey buds, shall ever equal.

I Think Continually of Those Who Were Truly Great

STEPHEN SPENDER

I think continually of those who were truly great.
Who, from the womb, remembered the soul's history
Through corridors of light where the hours are suns
Endless and singing. Whose lovely ambition
Was that their lips, still touched with fire,
Should tell of the Spirit clothed from head to foot in
song.
And who hoarded from the Spring branches
The desires falling across their bodies like blossoms.

What is precious is never to forget
The essential delight of the blood drawn from ageless
springs
Breaking through rocks in worlds before our earth.
Never to deny its pleasure in the morning simple light
Nor its grave evening demand for love.
Never to allow gradually the traffic to smother
With noise and fog the flowering of the spirit.

Near the snow, near the sun, in the highest fields
See how these names are fêted by the waving grass
And by the streamers of white cloud
And whispers of wind in the listening sky.

The names of those who in their lives fought for life
Who wore at their hearts the fire's centre.
Born of the sun they travelled a short while towards the
  sun,
And left the vivid air signed with their honour.

From All These Events, from the Slump, from the War, from the Boom

STEPHEN SPENDER

From all these events, from the slump, from the war,
  from the boom,
From the Italian holiday, from the skirring
Of the revolving light for an adventurer,
From the crowds in the square at dusk, from the shoot-
  ing,
From the loving, from the dying, however we prosper in
  death
Whether lying under twin lilies and branched candles
Or stiffened on the pavement like a frozen sack, hidden
From night and peace by the lamps:
From all these events: Time solitary will emerge
Like a rocket bursting from mist: above the trouble
Untangled with our pasts, be sure Time will leave us.

At first growing up in us more nakedly than our own
  nature
Driving us beyond what seemed the final choking swamp,
Ruin, the all-covering illness, to a new and empty air;
Singling us from the war which killed ten millions;
Carrying us elate through the happy summer fields;
Nesting us in high rooms of a house where voices
Murmured at night from the garden, as if flowering
  from water;

Then sending us to lean days after the years of fulfilment;
At last dropping us in the hard, bright crater of the dead.

Our universal ally, but larger than our purpose, whose flanks
Stretch to planets unknown in our brief, particular battle,
Tomorrow Time's progress will forget us even here,
When our bodies are rejected like the beetle's shard, today
Already, now, we are forgotten on those stellar shores.
Time's ambition, huge as space, will hang its flags
In distant worlds, and in years on this world as distant.

The Funeral

STEPHEN SPENDER

Death is another milestone on their way.
With laughter on their lips and with winds blowing round them
They record simply
How this one excelled all others in making driving belts.

This is festivity, it is the time of statistics
When they record what one unit contributed:
They are glad as they lay him back in the earth
And thank him for what he gave them.

They walk home remembering the straining red flags,
And with pennons of song still fluttering through their blood
They speak of the world state
With its towns like brain-centres and its pulsing arteries.

They think how one life hums, revolves and toils,
One cog in a golden and singing hive:
Like spark from fire, its task happily achieved,
It falls away quietly.

No more are they haunted by the individual grief
Nor the crocodile tears of European genius,
The decline of a culture
Mourned by scholars who dream of the ghosts of Greek
boys.

oh young men oh young comrades

STEPHEN SPENDER

oh young men oh young comrades
it is too late now to stay in those houses
your fathers built where they built you to build to breed
money on money it is too late
to make or even to count what has been made
Count rather those fabulous possessions
which begin with your body and your fiery soul:—
the hairs on your head the muscles extending
in ranges with their lakes across your limbs
Count your eyes as jewels and your valued sex
then count the sun and the innumerable coined light
sparkling on waves and spangled under trees
It is too late to stay in great houses where the ghosts are
  prisoned
—those ladies like flies perfect in amber
those financiers like fossils of bones in coal.
Oh comrades, step beautifully from the solid wall
advance to rebuild and sleep with friend on hill
advance to rebel and remember what you have
no ghost ever had, immured in his hall.

The Yachts

WILLIAM CARLOS WILLIAMS

contend in a sea which the land partly encloses
shielding them from the too heavy blows
of an ungoverned ocean which when it chooses

tortures the biggest hulls, the best man knows
to pit against its beating, and sinks them pitilessly.
Mothlike in mists, scintillant in the minute

brilliance of cloudless days, with broad bellying sails
they glide to the wind tossing green water
from their sharp prows while over them the crew crawls

ant-like, solicitously grooming them, releasing,
making fast as they turn, lean far over and having
caught the wind again, side by side, head for the mark.

In a well guarded arena of open water surrounded by
lesser and greater craft which, sycophant, lumbering
and flittering follow them, they appear youthful, rare

as the light of a happy eye, live with the grace
of all that in the mind is feckless, free and
naturally to be desired. Now the sea which holds them

is moody, lapping their glossy sides, as if feeling
for some slightest flaw but fails completely.
Today no race. Then the wind comes again. The yachts

move, jockeying for a start, the signal is set and they
are off. Now the waves strike at them but they are too
well made, they slip through, though they take in canvas.

Arms with hands grasping seek to clutch at the prows.
Bodies thrown recklessly in the way are cut aside.
It is a sea of faces about them in agony, in despair

until the horror of the race dawns staggering the mind,
the whole sea become an entanglement of watery bodies
lost to the world bearing what they cannot hold. Broken,

beaten, desolate, reaching from the dead to be taken up
they cry out, failing, failing! their cries rising
in waves still as the skillful yachts pass over.

Fallow Land

EUNICE CLARK

Fallow land, how low the crows fly!
A lady of the house remembers amour;
The phlox survive, but hay runs thin where there
Birnam Wood crosses the pasture bars.
There shall be murder tonight in Pittsburgh!
But here are rainsore roofs, here tools unsoldered,
Vines over the window, and bitterly
The rust assaulting and impertinent birds.
Close-packed fruit and eggs we used to send;
(The graveyard needs repair, the tombstones topple)
What are they eating now, the city people?
Kneel, lady of the house, and pray. Close
Over her, forest. Fallow land, avenge
Her memories
                    low flying crows.

The People Has No Obituary

EUNICE CLARK

Death cannot surprise us who are driven
Century after century through seas of men.
No drought of life is here, no person
Too rare to lose, who cannot be found again.

Partings are not final. No self is past changing
And replacing. Grains from a deep bin,
Male and female we are broadcast. Without ritual
Seed is severed from flower, kith from kin.

Death does not frighten us who read the notices
Of thousands dying. We have won
Only a number by our borning, and another
Long number when the sand has run.

Death is a word the rich love, keening
Over the precise career of a lost one.
We are the seed spent lavishly in cities:
We wander, mourning all but naming none.

Men, women in cities, multitudes, millions,
Receding, increasing without annual plan,
The people is the jungle-soil of heroes, flourishing
When death dries out the special planted man.

The Death of the Craneman

ALFRED HAYES

Happened like this: it was hot as hell
That afternoon, sand, stone dust, the sun,
We were in the mountains.
Drinking-water was by the gasoline drum
We were all drinking like fish that day.
He must have come down from the crane
For a drink I guess, a cigarette
Might have done it, blew it bang up, that drum,
Like dynamite been dropped in it.
We came running down from the mountains.
The blacksmith got to him first: gasoline
Had made a bonfire of him, and we shouted
Craneman! Craneman! with the wops talking
Their language, and nobody knowing his name.
Standing there you could see him, a flame
Lighter and yellower than the sunlight,
And burning, hands and feet, his hair on fire,
Getting up from the ground, standing there,
Yelling out of the fire, flame shooting white
In the sunlight: Lemme alone! Lemme alone!
I'm all right!

Well, we get him here and here he dies.
And that's where we buried him out there,
In the goldenrod beyond them pines.
It's a Potter's Field and nobody'd care.

We dug the grave with our drills and hands.
You got to bury a guy somewhere.
Funny I thought as I looked at him
Blackened, with a pair of holes for eyes,
You bury a stiff and there he lies,
And Christ only knows where he come from
And whether there's kids somewhere or a dame,
We buried him like he came in this world,
A stiff, naked, without a name.

Consuelo at the Country Club

SELDEN RODMAN

1.

Sharp triangles of red rubber and white
Intersect and are lost in the clean light
Where six brown bathers in the latest styles
Grouped in a regular hexagon like the tiles
Know they are watched by the eyes pouring tea
From the porch who hate with a chattering frenzy

The topic for discussion under the awning
Will save one man and seventeen women from yawning
Because if I miss my golf Where did you put it
Yes I received the bill He won't foot it
Why are his feet in the water If one must call
Tonight have you heard they're giving another ball

Consuelo from somewhere in the half dark
Of a door steps out in time to be the mark
Of the descending arm and eye of the suntanned
Bather the ball falls out and into the sand
She speaks and everyone speaks and someone is thrown
In the populous water you are suddenly alone

And lie for a long time separated
Remembering the hours before the porch debated

Furiously between the splash of the song
Was it right   yes   no   was it wrong
While bravely with that light it never earned
The moon's superior radiance burned

2.

Lighting a cigarette casually he glances
Her way to see if the light of her own enhances
That spire of recognition between her Spanish eyes
Faint as the twist of a knot before it vanishes
Wondering   is there anything left to matter
Now that love is guilt and truth chatter

My husband is in the city   come if you can
If you can't don't   who is the attractive man
Sitting between   my legs are still wet from the water
Or save the expense of a tea for your other daughter
Or save   I'll meet you beside the courts at twelve
I'll be there he lied   see that you're there yourself

So turned and dove in the water and rose
To the surface   pulled up   out   and into his clothes
Saw her again nodding pleasantly goodafternoon
To the ladies out of his eye in a different tone
Thinking   now or never   less cruel if quick
And left for ever   I wonder are both of them sick

Over their lives united and suddenly snapped
Built out of evenings and afternoons and now wrapped

In the city's quite impersonal distance
Beyond the women on the porch whose assistance
Consists of the infallible judgment of what is right
While watching sharp triangles of red rubber and white

3.

But put them together again now if you can
Seven years later by accident plan
To have them meet in a suburban station
Will there be more abandon in his recognition
Than the man on the platform whose passions fuse
His wife his ticket and the *Morning News*

Will Consuelo direct the play
Of her proper progeny as on that day
Each mother forgetting she was once undone
Directed her soon-to-be-important son
To dive for the penny before it sank
Keep it she said we will put it in the bank

And ladies does your Club still stand unshaken
Where the best people meet do the lesser waken
In the well-stocked cellars is the larder locked
Clay-pigeons poised and shotguns cocked
The courts still empty and the links sparse
But the drive still congested with enormous cars

Leave them remember the unguarded day
The chequered sunlight the unchecked play

The immortal music of the casual word
Unpremeditated   wrong   absurd
The deed in doing it   remember at night
The ball thrown nowhere and the bird in flight

From *Lawrence: The Last Crusade*

SELDEN RODMAN

Out of the East the plane spun; over rolling
Once fertile fields that swelled to birth of nations
And now are big with pain again, she banks
Upon the bar of Europe. Throttled lightly
Above the armies in the earth beneath her,
To catch what sound might rise to drown the drone
Of blades or burr of motors, nothing rises
To that clean eminence; nor mark of ages
By spark of shells is interrupted long,
Though seen by tired eyes, shifting and blinking,
Dazzled with too much light. At length she turns
By Adriatic archipelagos
That catch the sun, by sails, by gleaming beaches
The sea spawns; spinning, she sinks, leaps up and onward
And circling comes to rest.

*

These are the men who make avenging armies:
The freedom-fighters, riding over doubt
With spur and whip: unquestioning: possessors:
Blood on their hands, their faces cruel, like runners
All frozen stiff from straining at the distance:
Drained of morality, volition dry
In greed for victory, they blow like leaves
Before the body's death and mind's surrender:

Yea-sayers, faithful, asking "Where?" not "Why?"
They do not stop. No flower by the wayside
Attracts tomorrow-eyes that pierce today,
Nor wayward beauty; never can they remember,
Never reflect: the builders of the new
Must kill the old and kill themselves to conquer.
Blesséd inheritors!—But bless these too.

*

Increase the speed: increase it and increase it
To roar of ninety . . . ninety-five . . . one hundred . . .
Four thousand revolutions to the minute
Firing instantaneous: pistons slam
One hundred thirty power strokes a second.
To feel the shape of air, to strip the wind
With jets of ice in my dissolving eyes,
Carving the slipstream of my impetus;
To watch the gleaming roads unwind like tape,
The landscape hammer at my senses, be
Controlling, yet more uncontrollable
For accident, emergency unseen,
Than drifting leaf! Ah, this is liberty:
To laugh at death, to let the body race
Outstripping mind: these trees become one tree,
Small dingy homes one single shining home,
Fences dissolve, and ride until this world
Shall stretch as wide for every soul as here
This strip of sand, with hedge on every side . . .

Get There If You Can and See the Land You Once Were Proud to Own

W. H. AUDEN

Get there if you can and see the land you once were
  proud to own
Though the roads have almost vanished and the ex-
  presses never run:

Smokeless chimneys, damaged bridges, rotting wharves
  and choked canals,
Tramlines buckled, smashed trucks lying on their side
  across the rails;

Power-stations locked, deserted, since they drew the
  boiler fires;
Pylons fallen or subsiding, trailing dead high-tension
  wires;

Head-gears gaunt on grass-grown pit-banks, seams aban-
  doned years ago;
Drop a stone and listen for its splash in flooded dark
  below.

Squeeze into the works through broken windows or
  through damp-sprung doors;
See the rotted shafting, see holes gaping in the upper
  floors;

Where the Sunday lads come talking motor bicycle and
  girl,
Smoking cigarettes in chains until their heads are in a
  whirl.

Far from there we spent the money, thinking we could
  well afford,
While they quietly undersold us with their cheaper trade
  abroad;

At the theatre, playing tennis, driving motor cars we had,
In our continental villas, mixing cocktails for a cad.

These were boon companions who devised the legends
  for our tombs,
Those who have betrayed us nicely while we took them
  to our rooms.

Newman, Ciddy, Plato, Fronny, Pascal, Bowdler, Baudelaire,
Dr. Frommer, Mrs. Allom, Freud, the Baron, and Flau-
  bert.

Lured with their compelling logic, charmed with beauty
  of their verse,
With their loaded sideboards whispered 'Better join us,
  life is worse.'

Taught us at the annual camps arranged by the big business men
'Sunbathe, pretty till you're twenty. You shall be our servants then.'

Perfect pater. Marvellous mater. Knock the critic down who dares–
Very well, believe it, copy, till your hair is white as theirs.

Yours you say were parents to avoid, avoid then if you please
Do the reverse on all occasion till you catch the same disease.

When we asked the way to Heaven, these directed us ahead
To the padded room, the clinic and the hangman's little shed.

Intimate as war-time prisoners in an isolation camp,
Living month by month together, nervy, famished, lousy, damp.

On the sopping esplanade or from our dingy lodgings we
Stare out dully at the rain which falls for miles into the sea.

Lawrence, Blake and Homer Lane, once healers in our English land;
These are dead as iron for ever; these can never hold our hand.

Lawrence was brought down by smut-hounds, Blake went dotty as he sang,
Homer Lane was killed in action by the Twickenham Baptist gang.

Have things gone too far already? Are we done for? Must we wait
Hearing doom's approaching footsteps regular down miles of straight;

Run the whole night through in gumboots, stumble on and gasp for breath,
Terrors drawing close and closer, winter landscape, fox's death;

Or, in friendly fireside circle, sit and listen for the crash
Meaning that the mob has realized something's up, and start to smash;

Engine-drivers with their oil-cans, factory girls in overalls
Blowing sky-high monster stores, destroying intellectuals?

Hope and fear are neck and neck: which is it near the course's end
Crashes, having lost his nerve; is overtaken on the bend?

Shut up talking, charming in the best suits to be had
in town,
Lecturing on navigation while the ship is going down.

Drop those priggish ways for ever, stop behaving like a
stone:
Throw the bath-chairs right away, and learn to leave
ourselves alone.

If we really want to live, we'd better start at once to try;
If we don't, it doesn't matter, but we'd better start to
die.

Sir, No Man's Enemy, Forgiving All

W. H. AUDEN

Sir, no man's enemy, forgiving all
But will his negative inversion, be prodigal:
Send to us power and light, a sovereign touch
Curing the intolerable neural itch,
The exhaustion of weaning, the liar's quinsy,
And the distortions of ingrown virginity.
Prohibit sharply the rehearsed response
And gradually correct the coward's stance;
Cover in time with beams those in retreat
That, spotted, they turn though the reverse were great;
Publish each healer that in city lives
Or country house at the end of drives;
Harrow the house of the dead; look shining at
New styles of architecture, a change of heart.

The Airman's Alphabet

W. H. AUDEN

ACE–	Pride of parents and photographed person and laughter in leather.
BOMB–	Curse from cloud and coming to crook and saddest to steeple.
COCKPIT–	Soft seat and support of soldier and hold for hero.
DEATH–	Award for wildness and worst in the west and painful to pilots.
ENGINE–	Darling of designers and dirty dragon and revolving roarer.
FLYING–	Habit of hawks and unholy hunting and ghostly journey.

GAUGE–	Informer about oil and important to eye and graduated glass.
HANGAR–	Mansion of machine and motherly to metal and house of handshaking.
INSTRUMENT–	Dial on dashboard and destroyer of doubt and father of fact.
JOYSTICK–	Pivot of power and responder to pressure and grip for the glove.
KISS–	Touch taking off and tenderness in time and firmness on flesh.
LOOPING–	Flying folly and feat at fairs and brave to boys.
MECHANIC–	Owner of overalls and interested in iron and trusted with tools.

NOSE-DIVE– Nightmare to nerves
and needed by no one
and dash toward death.

OBSERVER– Peeper through periscope
and peerer at pasture
and eye in the air.

PROPELLER– Wooden wind-oar
and twisted whirler
and lifter of load.

QUIET– Absent from airmen
and easy to horses
and got in the grave.

RUDDER– Deflector of flight
and flexible fin
and pointer of path.

STORM– Night from the north
and numbness nearing
and hail ahead.

TIME– Expression of alarm
and used by the ill
and personal space.

UNDERCARRIAGE– Softener of shock
and seat on the soil
and easy to injure.

VICTIM– Corpse after crash
and carried through country
and atonement for aircraft.

WIRELESS– Sender of signal
and speaker of sorrow
and news from nowhere.

X– Mark upon map
and meaning mischief
and lovers' lingo.

YOUTH– Daydream of devils
and dear to the damned
and always to us.

ZERO– Love before leaving
and touch of terror
and time of attack.

Chorus from *The Dog Beneath the Skin*

W. H. AUDEN

(with Christopher Isherwood)

You with shooting-sticks and cases for field-glasses, your
limousines parked in a circle: who visit the public
games, observing in burberries the feats of the body:
You who stand before the west fronts of cathedrals: ap-
praising the curious carving:
The virgin creeping like a cat to the desert, the trumpet-
ing angels, the usurers boiling:
And you also who look for truth: alone in tower:
Follow our hero and his escort on his latest journey:
From the square surrounded by Georgian houses,
taking the lurching tram eastward
South of the ship-cranes, of the Slythe canal: stopping
at Fruby and Drulger Street,
Past boys ball-using: shrill in alleys.
Passing the cinemas blazing with bulbs: bowers of bliss
Where thousands are holding hands: they gape at the
tropical vegetation, at the Ionic pillars and the
organ solo.
Look left: The moon shows locked sheds, wharves by
water,
On your right is the Power House: its chimneys fume
gently above us like rifles recently fired.

Look through the grating at the vast machinery: at the dynamos and turbines
Grave, giving no sign of the hurricane of steam within their huge steel bottles,
At the Diesel engines like howdahed elephants: at the dials with their flickering pointers:
Power to the city: where loyalties are not those of the family.
And now, enter:
O human pity, gripped by the crying of a captured bird wincing at sight of surgeon's lance,
Shudder indeed: that life on its narrow littoral so lucky
Can match against eternity a time so cruel!
The street we enter with setts is paved: cracked and uneven as an Alpine glacier,
Garbage chucked in the gutters has collected in the hollows in loathsome pools,
Back to back houses on both sides stretch: a dead-straight line of dung-colored brick
Wretched and dirty as a run for chickens.
Full as a theatre is the foul thoroughfare: some sitting like sacks, some slackly standing,
Their faces grey in the glimmering gaslight: their eyeballs drugged like a dead rabbit's,
From a window a child is looking, by want so fretted his face has assumed the features of a tortoise:
A human forest: all by one infection cancelled.

Despair so far invading every tissue has destroyed in these the hidden seat of the desire and the intelligence.

A little further, and now: Enter the street of some of your dreams:
Here come the untidy jokers and the spruce who love military secrets
And those whose houses are dustless and full of Ming vases:
Those rebels who have freed nothing in the whole universe from the tyranny of the mothers, except a tiny sensitive area:
Those who are ashamed of their baldness or the size of their members,
Those suffering from self-deceptions necessary to life
And all who have compounded envy and hopelessness into desire
Perform here nightly their magical acts of identification
Among the Chinese lanterns and the champagne served in shoes.
You may kiss what you like; it has often been kissed before.
Use what words you wish; they will often be heard again.

Chorus from *The Ascent of F 6*

W. H. AUDEN

(with Christopher Isherwood)

At last the secret is out, as it always must come in the end;
The delicious story is ripe to tell to the intimate friend;
Over the tea cups and in the square the tongue has its desire;
Still waters run deep, my dear, there's never smoke without fire.
Behind the corpse in the reservoir, behind the ghost on the links,
Behind the lady who dances and the man who madly drinks,
Under the look of fatigue, the attack of migraine and the sigh
There is always another story, there is more than meets the eye.
For the clear voice suddenly singing, high up in the convent wall,
The scent in the elder bushes, the sporting prints in the hall,
The croquet matches in summer, the handshake, the cough, the kiss,
There is always a wicked secret, a private reason for this.

Prologue

W. H. AUDEN

O love, the interest itself in thoughtless Heaven,
Make simpler daily the beating of man's heart; within,
There in the ring where name and image meet,

Inspire them with such a longing as will make his thought
Alive like patterns a murmuration of starlings
Rising in joy over wolds unwittingly weave;

Here too on our little reef display your power,
This fortress perched on the edge of the Atlantic scarp,
The mole between all Europe and the exile-crowded sea;

And make us as Newton was, who in his garden watching
The apple falling toward England, became aware
Between himself and her of an eternal tie.

For now that dream which so long has contented our will,
I mean, of uniting the dead into a splendid empire,
Under whose fertilising flood the Lancashire moss

Sprouted up chimneys, and Glamorgan hid a life
Grim as a tidal rock-pool's in its glove-shaped valleys,
Is already retreating into her maternal shadow;

Leaving the furnaces gasping in the impossible air,
The flotsam at which Dumbarton gapes and hungers;
While upon wind-loved Rowley no hammer shakes

The cluster of mounds like a midget golf course, graves
Of some who created these intelligible dangerous marvels;
Affectionate people, but crude their sense of glory.

Far-sighted as falcons, they looked down another future;
For the seed in their loins were hostile, though afraid of their pride,
And, tall with a shadow now, inertly wait.

In bar, in netted chicken-farm, in lighthouse,
Standing on these impoverished constricting acres,
The ladies and gentlemen apart, too much alone,

Consider years of the measured world begun,
The barren spiritual marriage of stone and water.
Yet, O, at this very moment of our hopeless sigh

When inland they are thinking their thoughts but are watching these islands,
As children in Chester look to Moel Fammau to decide
On picnics by the clearness or withdrawal of her treeless crown,

Some possible dream, long coiled in the ammonite's
slumber
Is uncurling, prepared to lay on our talk and kindness
Its military silence, its surgeon's idea of pain;

And out of the Future, into actual History,
As when Merlin, tamer of horses, and his lords to whom
Stonehenge was still a thought, the Pillars passed

And into the undared ocean swung north their prow,
Drives through the night and star-concealing dawn
For the virgin roadsteads of our hearts an unwavering
keel.

Definition

EDWIN ROLFE

Knowing this man, who calls himself comrade
mean, underhanded, lacking all attributes
real men desire, that replenish all worlds
men strive for; knowing that charlatan, fool too,
masquerading always in our colors, must also
be addressed as comrade—knowing these
and others to be false, deficient in knowledge
and love for fellow men that motivates our kind,

nevertheless I answer the salutation proudly,
equally sure that no one can defile it,
feeling deeper than the word the love it bears,
the world it builds. And no man, lying,
talking behind back, betraying trustful friend,
is worth enough to soil this word or mar this world.

The Road from Election to Christmas

OSCAR WILLIAMS

The hurdy-gurdy, public piano of the past
Grinds out a thousand lithe cats on the autumn street;
The heart trembles like a lower lip
And memories crowd the doorway:
Out of the skyline, above the façades and the clocks,
The music box of the giant years
Drips its tinkling agonies about our ears:
The young, the newer moments steadily arrive:
The famous painting on the wall listens politely
But refuses to come alive . . .

Out of the belly of the public address system
Arises the speaker to people the evening air:
All wandering ears are now conscripted
On a dreadful march into the annals of winter:
You are now to hear pouring from all the crevices
Of the cracked voice, the revelations of despair—
From the water-tank perched on civilization's horizon
Flow the melted down, long overdue, fluid haloes
For the despoiled, the cheated and the badly bruised:
Fellow citizens, in what part of your anatomy
Do you hide your vote? Little bird inside the human
skin
Come forth: we have a worm for your beak:

It's a long unending worm, designed to choke you in the end . . .

The ocean slobbers on the shore, flapping slattern breakers,
But cannot confuse the issue
Nor wash away the brazen voice that hammers in the brain:
The election auctions off
The ornate sentiments, the burled thighs of the furniture;
The wooden pillars of society are taken from the files;
The evening becomes a lamp in the throat of silence,
And everywhere one can see on the streets
The black baleful cocked eyes of the loudspeakers
Like spies out of the subconscious surveying the age:
Mr. Voter, the bread you have been eating is wormy
With blackguards: look at his record: our worthy opponent
Is handing out alphabet soup in the kitchens of his mind:
Don't be fooled any longer: salvation has both
Her arms around your neck: we appeal to the highest
In your lower instincts . . .

The radio cracks its whip, the election shifts,
The glacier moves, elbowing into the foaming forest:
The brain splits open: the victor crams the headlines
Hurriedly into his mouth, and a sound of eating
Disturbs the polite conversation: the loser

Sits on an ice floe, his friends scampering in the horizon:
The rock of ages falls and spreads the citizen
Into his three dimensions: the election is over:
That bear, the people, eats honey in the dark:
Time now to clean the ticker-tape from the clover,
The pamphlets and buttons from the violated park:
No need to fear the fear of fear,
The road to Christmas is clear.

The Elements

OSCAR WILLIAMS

Above the hemispheres there floats
A melody both strange and rare
Where aeroplanes like molten notes
Fall on the mammoth ear of air.

Over the seven vibrant seas
The giant hand of commerce dips
Touching the morrow's harmonies
With steamships for its fingertips.

With forges in its throat, fire clangs
And bellows paean to the light;
Then chasing setting suns, it hangs
Its neon necklaces on night.

And through the ancient earth there moves
Amazing music, canyon-deep,
Where under the momentous hooves
The ivory flames of granite leap,

As down this morning of mankind
Through winding valleys of events,
Man blows the golden horn of mind
And hunts beside his elements.

From *Dusk of the Gods*

S. FUNAROFF

Of my deep hunger
great dreams grew,
and I made of my ideal
my bread.

I stopped my tears
and God's wells ran dry,
of my disbelief
a desert bloomed.

I made of the truth
my sword of need,
I made of my anger
a battlefield;

and in my need
I knew no fear:
I swung my hammer,
their structures fell.

I stopped my labor,
machines were still,
and I made of their laws
a broken staff.

I drove the lender
from the land.
I gave the tiller
back his soil.
I gave the toiler
back his toil.

My field of war
was a growing field
where all my victories
were sown,

and I made of my joy
a harvest's yield.
My joy, it rose,
a new-found land.

Reflections in an Iron works

HUGH MAC DIARMID

Would you resembled the metal you work with,
Would the iron entered into your souls,
Would you became like steel on your own behalf!
You are still only putty that tyranny rolls
Between its fingers! You makers of bayonets and guns
For your own destruction! No wonder that those
Weapons you make turn on you and mangle and
  murder—
You fools who equip your otherwise helpless foes!

At the Cenotaph

HUGH MAC DIARMID

Are the living so much use
That we need to mourn the dead?
Or would it yield better results
To reverse their roles instead?
The millions slain in the War—
Untimely, the best of our seed?—
Would the world be any the better
If they were still living indeed?
The achievements of such as are
To the notion lend no support;
The whole history of life and death
Yields no scrap of evidence for't.—
Keep going to your wars, you fools, as of yore;
I'm the civilization you're fighting for.

For One Who Would Not Take His Life in His Hands

DELMORE SCHWARTZ

Athlete, virtuoso,
Training for happiness,
Bend arm and knee, and seek
The body's sharp distress;
For pain is pleasure's cost,
Denial is the route
To speech before the millions
Or personal with the flute.

The ape and great Achilles,
Heavy with their fate,
Batter doors down, strike
Small children at the gate;
Driven by love to this,
As knock-kneed Hegel said,
To seek with a sword for peace
That the child may be lifted from
The recent dead.

"Ladies and Gentlemen," said
The curious Socrates,
"I have asked: What is this life
But a childermass,

As Abraham recognized,
A working with the knife
At animal, maid, and stone
Until we have cut down
All but the soul alone:
Through hate we come to love,
No other means is known."

City of Monuments

MURIEL RUKEYSER

Washington, 1934

Be proud   you people   of these graves
   these chiseled words   this precedent
From these blind ruins shines our monument.

Dead navies of the brain will sail
   stone celebrate its final choice
   when the air shakes, a single voice
a strong voice able to prevail:

Entrust no hope to stone although the stone
shelter the root: see too-great burdens placed
with nothing certain but the risk
set on the infirm column of
the high memorial obelisk

erect in accusation sprung against
a barren sky taut over Anacostia:

give over, Gettysburg! a word will shake your glory:
blood of the starved fell thin upon this plain,
this battle is not buried with its slain.

   Gravestone and battlefield retire
   the whole green South is shadowed dark,

the slick white domes are cast in night.
But uneclipsed above the park

the veteran of the Civil War
sees havoc in the tended graves
the midnight bugles blown to free
still unemancipated slaves.

Blinded by chromium or transfiguration
we watch, as through a miscroscope, decay:
down the broad streets the limousines
advance in passions of display.

Air glints with diamonds, and these clavicles
emerge through orchids by whose trailing spoor
the sensitive cannot mistake
the implicit anguish of the poor.

The throats incline, the marble men rejoice
careless of torrents of despair.

Split by a tendril of revolt
stone cedes to blossom everywhere.

The Trial

MURIEL RUKEYSER

The South is green with coming spring; revival
flourishes in the fields of Alabama. Spongy with rain,
plantations breathe April: carwheels suck mud in the
    roads,
the town expands warm in the afternoons. At night the
    black boy
teeters no-handed on a bicycle, whistling The St. Louis
    Blues,
blood beating, and hot South. A red brick courthouse
is vicious with men inviting death. Array your judges;
                                        call your jurors; come,
here is your justice, come out of the crazy jail.
Grass is green now in Alabama; Birmingham dusks are
    quiet
relaxed and soft in the park, stern at the yards:
a hundred boxcars shunted off to sidings, and the hoboes
gathering grains of sleep in forbidden corners.
In all the yards: Atlanta, Chattanooga,
Memphis, and New Orleans, the cars, and no jobs.

Every night the mail-planes burrow the sky,
carrying postcards to laughing girls in Texas,
passionate letters to the Charleston virgins,
words through the South: and no reprieve,
no pardon, no release.

A blinded statue attends before the courthouse,
bronze and black men lie on the grass, waiting,
the khaki dapper National Guard leans on its bayonets.
But the air is populous beyond our vision:
all the people's anger finds its vortex here
as the mythic lips of justice open, and speak.

Hammers and sickles are carried in a wave of strength,
    fire-tipped,
swinging passionately ninefold to a shore.
Answer the back-thrown Negro face of the lynched, the
    flat forehead knotted,
the eyes showing a wild iris, the mouth a welter of
    blood,
answer the broken shoulders and these twisted arms.
John Brown, Nat Turner, Toussaint stand in this court-
    room,
Dred Scott wrestles for freedom there in the dark corner,
all our celebrated shambles are repeated here: now
    again
Sacco and Vanzetti walk to a chair, to the straps and
    rivets
and the switch spitting death and Massachusetts' will.
Wreaths are brought out of history
  here are the well-nourished flowers of France, grown
    strong on blood,
  Caesar twisting his thin throat toward conquest,
    turning north from the Roman laurels,
  the Istrian galleys slide again to sea.

How they waded through bloody Godfrey's Jerusalem!
How the fires broke through Europe, and the rich
and the tall jails battened on revolution!
The fastidious Louis', cousins to the sun, stamping
those ribboned heels on Calas, on the people;
the lynched five thousand of America.
Tom Mooney from San Quentin, Herndon: here
is an army for audience

all resolved

to a gobbet of tobacco, spat, and the empanelled hundred,
a jury of vengeance, the cheap pressed lips, the narrow eyes like hardware;
the judge, his eye-sockets and cheeks dark and immutably secret,
the twisting mouth of the prosecuting attorney.

Nine dark boys spread their breasts against Alabama,
schooled in the cells, fathered by want.
Mother: one writes: they treat us bad. If they send us back to Kilby jail, I think I shall kill myself. I think I must hang myself by my overalls.

Alabama and the South are soft with spring;
in the North, the seasons change, sweet April, December and the air
loaded with snow. There is time for meetings
during the years, they remaining in prison.

a crowd listens, carrying banners.
Overhead, boring through the speaker's voice, a plane
circles with a snoring of motors revolving in the sky,
drowning the single voice. It does not touch
the crowd's silence. It circles. The name stands:
Scottsboro

Homage to Literature

MURIEL RUKEYSER

When you imagine trumpet-faced musicians
blowing again inimitable jazz
no art can accuse nor cannonadings hurt,
or coming out of your dreams of dirigibles
again see the unreasonable cripple
throwing his crutch headlong as the headlights

streak down the torn street, as the three hammerers
go One, Two, Three on the stake, triphammer pound-
    ings
and not a sign of new worlds to still the heart;

then stare into the lake of sunset as it runs
boiling, over the west past all control
rolling and swamps the heartbeat and repeats
sea beyond sea after unbearable suns;
think: poems fixed this landscape: Blake, Donne, Keats.

Boy with His Hair Cut Short

MURIEL RUKEYSER

Sunday shuts down on this twentieth-century evening.
The L passes. Twilight and bulb define
the brown room, the overstuffed plum sofa,
the boy, and the girl's thin hands above his head.
A neighbor's radio sings stocks, news, serenade.

He sits at the table, head down, the young clear neck
exposed,
watching the drugstore sign from the tail of his eye;
tattoo, neon, until the eye blears, while his
solicitous tall sister, simple in blue, bending
behind him, cuts his hair with her cheap shears.

The arrow's electric red always reaches its mark,
successful neon! He coughs, impressed by that precision.
His child's forehead, forever protected by his cap,
is bleached against the lamplight as he turns head
and steadies to let the snippets drop.

Erasing the failure of weeks with level fingers,
she sleeks the fine hair, combing: "You'll look fine
tomorrow!
You'll surely find something, they can't keep turning
you down;

the finest gentleman's not so trim as you!" Smiling, he raises
the adolescent forehead wrinkling ironic now.

He sees his decent suit laid out, new-pressed,
his carfare on the shelf. He lets his head fall, meeting
her earnest hopeless look, seeing the sharp blades splitting,
the darkened room, the impersonal sign, her motion,
the blue vein, bright on her temple, pitifully beating.

Citation for Horace Gregory

MURIEL RUKEYSER

These are our brave, these with their hands in on the
  work,
hammering out beauty upon the painful stone
turning their grave heads passionately finding
truth and alone and each day subtly slain
and each day born.
          Revolves
a measured system, world upon world, stemmed fires
and regulated galaxies behind the flattened head,
behind the immortal skull, ticking eternity
in blood and the symbols of living.

The brass voice speaks in the street
                    STRIKE STRIKE
  the nervous fingers continue elaborately
  drawing consciousness, examining, doing.
Rise to a billboard world of Chesterfields,
Mae West hip-wriggles, Tarzan prowess, the little
nibbling and despicable minds.
                Here, gentlemen,
here is our gallery of poets:
              Jeffers,
a long and tragic drum-roll beating anger,
sick of a catapulting nightmare world,
Eliot, who lead us to the precipice

subtly and perfectly; there striking an attitude
rigid and ageing on the penultimate step,
the thoughtful man MacLeish who bent his head
feeling the weight of the living; bent, and turned
the grave important face round to the dead.

And on your left, ladies and gentlemen: poets.

Young poets and makers, solve your anguish, see
the brave unmedalled, who dares to shape his mind,
printed with dignity, to the machines of change.
A procession of poets adds one footbeat to the
implacable metric line: the great and unbetrayed
   after the sunlight and the failing yellow,
   after the lips bitten with passion and
   gentle, after the deaths, below
   dance-floors of celebration   we turn   we turn
these braveries are permanent. These gifts
flare on our lives, clarifying, revealed.

We are too young to see our funerals
in pantomime nightly before uneasy beds,
too near beginnings for this hesitation
obliterated in death or carnival.
Deep into time extend the impersonal stairs,
   established barricades will stand,
before they die the brave have set their hand
on rich particular beauty for their heirs.

APPENDIX

BIOGRAPHICAL NOTES

JAMES AGEE was born in Knoxville, Tennessee, in 1909. His first book, with a foreword by Archibald MacLeish was published in 1934 by the Yale University Press. Its title, *Permit Me Voyage,* is taken from the last line of one of Hart Crane's "Voyages." After graduation from Harvard in 1932 Agee came to New York, joining that remarkable coterie of poets and free-thinkers, the editorial staff of *Fortune.* His verse, ornate as any Elizabethan's, is invariably sharp and pungent with an imagery struck from contemporary flint.

CONRAD AIKEN, equally distinguished as poet, critic and anthologist, was born in Georgia in 1889. After graduation from Harvard, he lived in Massachusetts until 1921; thereafter, until very recently, in Sussex, England. His novels, like his poems, are concerned with psychological problems. The mood, generally, is nostalgic. His *Selected Poems,* 1929, was awarded the Pulitzer Prize.

W. H. AUDEN is the strongest and most versatile member of that younger generation of English poets, including Spender and Day Lewis, which first made its voice heard at Oxford. He was born in 1907; has taught school; consistently been a radical; done journalistic service for the Spanish Loyalist and Chinese causes; received the King's Prize for poetry in 1937 from George VI. His style, the equipment of a major poet, is a highly personal blend of

Byronic wit and clinical precision; yet when he wishes to (witness the poem "Prologue") he can employ rhetoric in the grand manner. In addition to his poems, and his plays (with Christopher Isherwood), Auden is the co-editor of a most stimulating recent anthology, *The Poet's Tongue,* and of the entertaining travel-diary, *Letters from Iceland* (with Louis MacNeice).

STEPHEN VINCENT BENÉT, born in Bethlehem, Pennsylvania, in 1898, published a vigorous collection of poetic monologues, *Five Men and Pompey,* before he entered Yale in 1916. Producing in quick succession novels, ballads and short stories, he made a great name for himself in 1928 with the appearance of the novel-length narrative poem *John Brown's Body.* Although perhaps the most popular poem of our time (it has sold 169,000 copies and is still selling), *John Brown's Body* does not contain its author's best work—that combination of metrical experiment, elfish humor and social indignation which make *Burning City,* 1936, memorable.

WILLIAM ROSE BENÉT, the elder brother of Stephen Vincent, was born in 1886 and graduated from Yale in 1907. He served in the War, and in 1924 helped to found the *Saturday Review of Literature* of which he is still the poetry editor. In addition to his poetry (the most characteristic experiments and ballads are to be found in the collection *Man Possessed,* 1927), Benét edited the posthumous *Collected Poems* of his second wife, Elinor Wylie.

ROBERT BRIDGES, born in England in 1844 and educated at Oxford, was Poet Laureate from 1913 until his death in 1930. His lyrics, as well as his ambitious long poem, *The Testament of Beauty*, are distinguished by their conventional, pietistic subject-matter, and by a style, which, though subtle, is so deliberately patterned after classical models as to approach pedantry. He discovered Gerard Manley Hopkins in the 80's without fully understanding his genius, and edited the first collection of that poet's work.

RUPERT BROOKE died in 1915 at the age of 27. He was on his way to the Dardanelles after war service in Belgium. His romantic war poems, superficial, histrionic, are a sharp contrast to those of Wilfred Owen. Take the familiar

> If I should die, think only this of me;
> That there's some corner of a foreign field
> That is forever England . . .

Handsome, young, athletic, with warm, generous impulses, he was blotted out by one of the War's minor accidents before his talents matured.

ROY CAMPBELL was born in Natal, South Africa, in 1902. A latter-day Byron, the violence of *The Flaming Terrapin,* the satire of *The Georgiad,* the symbolism of *Adamastor* never quite come off. If a stricter discipline and larger purpose can mould a more individual style, Campbell may yet startle the world for he has the vitality of a major poet.

LEWIS CARROLL, the pen-name of the mathematician, C. L. Dodgson, is as well known to the world as his masterpiece, *Alice in Wonderland.* He was born in Cheshire, England, in 1832 and died in 1898. The immortal nonsense rhyme included in this volume has contributed at least four new words of common usage to the language—and it is still a treasury.

EUNICE CLARK (Mrs. John Knox Jessup) was born in New York City in 1911 and spent her childhood in Roxbury, Connecticut. The granddaughter of John Bates Clark, classic American economist and teacher of Veblen, she graduated from Vassar College in 1933 where she edited the *Vassar Miscellany News*. Since 1936 she has been a member of the editorial staff of *Fortune*. Her poems, symbolist in technique but always acutely social, have appeared in *Poetry, Common Sense,* the *Nation* and the *New Republic.*

SARAH N. CLEGHORN was born in 1876 at Norfolk, Virginia. She lives near Manchester, Vermont. She spent a year at Radcliffe, has taught at Manumit School and Vassar College, and her poems have appeared during the last thirty years everywhere from the old *Masses* and the *American* to the *Atlantic Monthly* and *Century*. Robert Frost, in his introduction to her autobiography, *Threescore,* contends that there is more "high explosive for righteousness" in a single line of Sarah Cleghorn's famous poem about the golf links than in the prose that labors under "several atmospheres of revolution." It originally appeared in 1915 in Franklin P. Adams' column in the *Tribune*.

MALCOLM COWLEY was born in the mining country of Pennsylvania in 1898. After his years at Harvard he went abroad with the earlier "exiles," edited *Secession,* contributed to *Broom* and *transition*. Better known as a critic and as literary editor of the *New Republic,* Cowley's poems (*Blue Juniata,* 1929) record the moods and attitudes of the Lost Generation far more profoundly than the autobiographical *Exile's Return*.

HART CRANE was born in Ohio in 1899. His integrity as an artist contrasted always—was perhaps the function of his inability to reconcile himself with his family and with society. His poetry, from the "imagism" of "Sunday Morning Apples" to the only partially successful myth-making of *The Bridge,* is difficult in proportion to its prodigious ambition and to its author's failure to find any resolution for his personal conflicts. But the grandeur of lines like

For joy rides in stupendous coverings

has not been rivalled in our time. Crane leapt into the Atlantic from the stern of the *S.S. Orizaba* in 1932. He was returning from the terrible sojourn in Mexico he describes so poignantly in "Purgatorio." His poetry, as well as his life, are analyzed in that paragon of what a poet's biography should be, *Hart Crane* by Philip Horton.

E. E. CUMMINGS, born in 1894, educated but not tamed at Harvard, first achieved celebrity among the discriminating with his powerful war novel, *The Enormous Room.* After years abroad, Cummings returned to live in New York and Vermont. His poetry, recently collected in a single volume, is well described by Louis Untermeyer as "a jumble of imaginative exuberance, cool precision and archaic affectations. His is a mind which is in quick succession, lyrical, fantastic, grotesque, pathetic, savage." It should be said in addition that Cummings is a first-rate humorist, and, despite his unabating eccentricity, one of the most original lyrical talents at work today. His description of Soviet Russia, *Eimi,* 1933, was a shock to those who hoped his literary iconoclasm would feel at home in Moscow.

WALTER DE LA MARE, born in 1873 in Kent, England, must spend a good part of his life in dread of the next anthologist who will neglect a hundred equally worthy poems to reprint "The Listeners." What irony, that the poem the Romantics and masters of neo-Gothic mystery never quite wrote, should have been finally achieved by a man who spent eighteen years of his life working for the Standard Oil Company! Equally renowned for his children's verse (*Peacock Pie,* etc.) and the novel (*Memoirs of a Midget*), De La Mare's poetry is notable for the subtlety with which its archaic diction and floating rhythms convey a spectral beauty.

T. S. ELIOT was born in 1888 in St. Louis and educated at Harvard and Oxford. The radical symbolist experimentor of "Prufrock," "Gerontion" and *The Waste Land,* after living in England two decades described himself as "classicist in literature, royalist in politics, Anglo-Catholic in religion." But if Eliot has become thrice subdued, in keeping with the pedantic perfection of his later verse and the schoolmasterly dogmatism of his essays, he has not by any means gone to sleep. His championship of younger talent in "The Criterion," the power of his popular verse-drama, *Murder in the Cathedral,* are answer enough to those who have prematurely written his obituary. Prophet of frustration, later of sophisticated piety, the artist remains master throughout. The philosophies, even the ornate style studded with literary allusion and quotation, may date quickly. The word-magic of poems like "The Hollow Men" and "Sweeney Among the Nightingales" is deathless.

PAUL ENGLE was born in Cedar Rapids, Iowa, in 1910; studied at the University of Iowa, Columbia and Oxford. His first book, *American Song,* was highly praised; his second, *Break the Heart's Anger,* roundly thumped. So far, Engle has been the slave of his own exuberance. He has attempted the difficult task of carrying the Whitman-Sandburg tradition into a generation socially rebellious and nurtured on symbolism. But he has thrown both shoes at the latter without re-appearing in adequate footwear of his own.

KENNETH FEARING, born in Chicago in 1902, worked as a millhand and journalist until the publication of his first book of poems, *Angel Arms,* in 1929. Already original for his kaleidoscopic realism, the development of *Poems,* 1935, may be appreciated by comparing the introductory poem of Part IV in this anthology with the later "Dirge." Whether the virtuosity of Fearing's bludgeoning manner will mature to a broader idiom is one of the important question-marks of "post-depression" poetry.

ARCHIBALD FLEMING was born in 1911. At Princeton in 1931 he collaborated on the undergraduate prize play. In literary affairs he has dropped his family name for obvious reasons—it happens to be MacLiesh. Since the publication of *The Island Called Pharos* in 1934, Fleming has lived in New City, N. Y. and devoted his talents to the writing of drama in verse. His poetry, though still unknown outside of a small circle, is distinguished by its skillful adaptations of symbolist rhythms to modern, especially scientific, material, and by a strange, almost other-worldly integrity.

ROBERT FROST, the poet *par excellence* of New England and already a classic in his own country, continues to create with unflagging distinction though his philosophy and style seem static. He was born in San Francisco in 1875 and was, off and on, a shoemaker, textile worker, student (Dartmouth and Harvard), teacher, editor, farmer—and unappreciated poet. His fame, when it came, was great, and has remained so. It began in England, where he lived from 1912 to 1915. Frost's poetry is precise, sly, meditative, sympathetic; always bucolic and generally didactic in a transcendental but conversational sort of way. He has described himself as one of two kinds of realist: not the kind "who offers a good deal of dirt with his potato to show that it is a real one," but rather "the one who is satisfied with the potato brushed clean."

S. FUNAROFF was born in 1911 and lives in New York City. He has worked as an upholsterer's apprentice, publicity man and Home Relief investigator. He has edited a poetry magazine, published (Dynamo Press) the first books of several younger poets, and collected outstanding verse by Federal writers for the *New Republic* and the *New Masses.* In 1933 he edited *We Gather Strength* and in 1935 served on the staff of *New Theatre.* His first book, *The Spider and the Clock,* was published in 1938 by International Publishers.

ARTHUR GUITERMAN was born in Vienna, Austria, in 1871 and graduated from the College of the City of New York in 1891. He has taught and lectured on poetry, and lives in Vermont. Author of *Death and General Putnam, Gaily the Troubadour,* etc., his light verse is distinguished by its sentimental lilting quality, and, at its best, by a felicitous humor.

HORACE GREGORY was born in Wisconsin in 1898, attended the University there, and lives in New York. A man of letters in the full creative sense—urban, Irish, full of a restless, generous energy—he almost neglects his poetry in the occupation of criticism and in a championship of younger talent that is unrivalled in contemporary America.

His lyrical gift, tempered by a strong sense of social injustice and disorder, reached maturity in *No Retreat,* 1933. But his elliptical philosophic verse (*Chorus for Survival,* 1935), his translations from Catullus, his critique of D. H. Lawrence's symbolism (*Pilgrim of the Apocalypse*) are equally fresh and vigorous. His wife, Marya Zaturenska, is a lyric poet celebrated in her own right. (Randolph Bourne, whose courageous career is celebrated in Gregory's second poem of this collection, was the crippled editor of the *New Republic* who fought a single-handed intellectual battle against America's entrance into the World War.)

THOMAS HARDY was born near Dorchester, England, in 1840. He died in 1928. Renowned as a novelist, the author of *The Return of the Native* and *Tess of the D'Urbervilles,* his first and last love was poetry, and to poetry went the essence of his homely genius. His verse has been criticized as harsh, its philosophy as fatalistic. It is the harshness of a giant's uncompromising strength, the fatalism of one who loved humanity too well to tell it pretty fables.

ALFRED HAYES was born in London, England, in 1911, but has lived in New York City 22 of his 27 years. He has worked as a reporter on a tabloid, for the WPA Federal Theatre's "Living Newspapers," and has contributed verse to the *New Masses, Trial Balances* and the *New Republic.* The influence of Browning, and possibly Masters, may be felt in the powerful "Death of the Craneman," but these are healthy influences today and Hayes has made the resultant style his own.

GERARD MANLEY HOPKINS may be fated, through the sheer intensity of his vision, to remain a poet's poet, though it is difficult to see how such a translucent poem as

"Pied Beauty" will escape the anthologies of the future. He was born in 1844, spent most of his life as a Jesuit priest and teacher of Greek metrics. He died in 1898. His poems, first published by Bridges in 1919, only achieved influence with the second edition of 1930. If Hopkins' style still appears difficult it is because, as one of his editors has said, his is "a passionate emotion which seems to try to utter all its words in one," and an equally passionate intellect "striving at once to recognize and explain both the singleness and division of the accepted universe. . . Others have sung *about* their intellectual exaltations; in none has the intellect itself been more the song." In addition to Hopkins' collected poems, the reader should not miss his superb letters, and the recently published *Note-Books and Papers* with reproductions of his exquisite Leonardo-like pen drawings.

A. E. HOUSMAN has compared poetry to a secretion: "whether a natural secretion, like turpentine in the fir, or a morbid secretion, like the pearl in the oyster." It is to the latter that one must turn for explanation of the pessimistic spell of *The Shropshire Lad.* Housman was born in 1859, and with the exception of the echo of *Last Poems* 30 years later, this slender sheaf was his only contribution to poetry in the 78 years of his life. It was a great contribution, and immediately popular, but the scholarly editor of Manilius' forgotten works made a fetish of his shattered inspiration, preferring to comment acidly in Latin upon the foibles of another day than to trust himself again to the buffetings of an uncloistered world. It was the world's misfortune, perhaps, that this perfectionist in a minor key who had succeeded in stripping poetry to the bone merely in linking the moods of adolescent melancholy and good cheer, should have been assured immortality before he was 40.

ROBINSON JEFFERS was born in Pittsburgh in 1887. He spent some of his youth abroad, but has lived most of his life in the tower he built for himself on the cliff above Carmel, California. He has been aptly described by William Harlan Hale as a latter-day Whitman, looking outward from the Pacific coast, rather than inward from the Atlantic, toward death rather than toward life. The sweep of Whitman is in his majestic verse, but the love has turned to hate, at best to pity and disgust. "Roan Stallion" was one of the first, and remains the best of that succession of long poems in which Jeffers celebrates the introversion of the race, usually through the symbol of incestuous, self-destructive love.

JOSEPHINE W. JOHNSON, author of the Pulitzer-Prize-winning *Now in November* and several other novels, was born in 1910 in Missouri and attended Washington University where she studied painting. She lives on a farm in St. Louis County and is active in union organizing work. Her poetry, while conventional in style, is remarkable for its emotional honesty and the sinew with which it handles social issues.

JAMES JOYCE, like another major novelist, the author of *Wuthering Heights,* is a minor poet, but a fine one. He was born in Dublin in 1882 and has lived in Zurich and Trieste and Paris since the days before the War. With the publication of *Ulysses* by Sylvia Beach in 1922, worshippers and imitators, charlatans and censors, perched on his doorstep and he became a legend. In Joyce's poetry, the lyricism of his prose is attenuated to a flute-like key, not often stirring and tragic as in "I Hear An Army," but full of sentiment, subdued and like the title of his first book, *Chamber Music.*

D. H. LAWRENCE was born in 1885 in the mining country of England and died in Nice, France, in 1930 after a tortured life spent wandering through Italy and Germany, Arizona and Mexico. What he sought—the 'noble savage,' masculine civilization, sex unperverted by guilt of mind or war of wills—he never found. His works, marred by a self-conscious sense of liberation and the zeal to convert or castigate, but burning with the intensity of his quest, are the result. The poems suffer more than the novels from the hysteria of the propagandist who will stop for no formal discipline; but poet and novelist are equal parts of the man, and at their best equally great. "The Ship of Death," found in a number of versions in his papers after his death, is Lawrence's last poem.

C. DAY LEWIS was born in Ireland in 1904 and educated at Oxford with Auden, Spender, Rex Warner and others of that younger group for whom he was to become the most articulate spokesman. His verse is more studied and programmatic than theirs, but his versatility (he is the author of several novels and is a first-rate critic) have won him deservedly equal rank.

VACHEL LINDSAY was born in Springfield, Illinois, in 1879. One of the most characteristic yet individual of American poets, he tramped the country, "bringing beauty to the people," inventing a popular music for its raucous blend of megalomania and idealism, selling his poems for bread, chanting from platforms like any other revivalist, exhausting himself and his art in one grand, generous splurge of emotion. There is Lindsay the prophet. There is Lindsay the crank; Lindsay the weaver of delicate phantasies for children; Lindsay the indignant Socialist. He may not have realized his goal of a "communal art," but he came closer to celebrating his country in terms that its people could appreciate than any other contemporary. He died in 1931.

PARE LORENTZ, born in West Virginia in 1905, attended West Virginia Wesleyan and served for a time as motion picture critic on such magazines as *Judge, Vanity Fair* and *McCalls.* He has written and directed two great documentary films, *The Plow That Broke The Plains* and *The River.* It was the second of these, produced by the Farm Security Administration, that was hailed as a new literary form when the book, combining soundtrack and pictures, appeared. Archibald MacLeish (in *Land of the Free*) and Erskine Caldwell and Margaret Bourke-White (*You Have Seen Their Faces*) had anticipated this development; but Lorentz's open-space cadences are a unique contribution to the Whitman tradition.

AMY LOWELL, of the Boston Lowells, but who smoked cigars and shocked her contemporaries even more with her free verse, was born in 1874 in Brookline, Mass. Renowned for her promotion of the imagist movement, she was an able craftswoman and a healthy influence in the 1912–20 renaissance, but her poetry, with little but its chromium finish to recommend it, seems dated today. Her two-volume life of Keats is still the standard biography. She died in 1925.

ARCHIBALD MAC LEISH was born in 1892. He graduated from Yale, where he excelled as scholar and athlete, and began the practice of law in Boston after attending the Harvard Law School. He had already seen war service in France and published one book of verse. Abandoning law, MacLeish travelled in France and Persia during the 20's, finally joining the editorial staff of *Fortune* where he is considered the ablest chronicler of the nation's industrial and political affairs. As a modern poet, MacLeish is one of the few who have never repeated themselves. Invariably, following his apprenticeship to Robinson, Eliot and the later French symbolists, he has written with distinction. From *The Hamlet of A. MacLeish* to the lyrics of *New Found Land* and the nostalgic *Conquistador* in narrative terza-rima, through the social satire of *Frescoes* and the trail-blazing radio play, *The Fall of the City,* MacLeish has developed as a poet, at the same time marking new ways, until today he is a generally acknowledged leader in the generation twenty years his junior.

LOUIS MAC NEICE was born in Ireland in 1907 and attended Oxford. A close friend of Auden, and the Oxford poets generally, he has gone his own way from the beginning, eschewing politics and beating out a somewhat crabbed but powerful style of his own. Satire is the prevailing weather in his landscapes. Spare solidity characterizes his authentic translation of Aeschylus' *Agamemnon.*

EDWIN MARKHAM was born in Oregon in 1852 and now lives in Staten Island, New York. No poem ever published in America has had the instant and lasting popularity of "The Man with the Hoe" which appeared in 1899. Conventional in form, inspired by the still more conventional Millet painting, its indignation and rugged strength are still challenging.

JOHN MASEFIELD, the present Poet Laureate of England, was born in 1878 and won an early fame with *Salt-Water Ballads* and the narratives, *Dauber* and *The Widow in the Bye Street.* The rude sincerity of his early work and the quotable lilt of such "anthology pieces" as "Cargoes" and "Sea Fever" are still prized above the magnificent narrative sweep of *Reynard the Fox*.

EDGAR LEE MASTERS was born in Kansas in 1869. As a realistic, psychological "novelist," if not as a poet, he takes his place beside Dreiser, Anderson and Dos Passos. For *Spoon River Anthology,* contributing little to the musical and architectural in poetry, remains a masterpiece of collective characterization. Neither ingratiating nor epigrammatic, Masters' weapon is blunt, effective.

HUGH MAC DIARMID is the pen-name of Christopher M. Grieve, a Scotsman born in 1892 and educated at Edinburgh University. As a student he joined the Fabian Society. Throughout the War he served in the Medical Corps, refusing to accept rank. As a Socialist, after the War, he helped to found the National Party of Scotland, from which he was subsequently expelled as a Communist. In 1936 he was expelled from the Communist Party for demanding Scottish autonomy, but was reinstated the same year. His "recreation" is given in the English *Who's Who* as "Anglophobia" and he now lives in one of the northernmost of the Shetland Islands. Much of Macdiarmid's poetry is in the Scots vernacular, and he has been compared to Robert Burns for the national-proletarian bite of his scurrilous lyrics. He is at his worst when he gets literary about "the eternal lightning of Lenin's bones"; at his best when he writes straight, letting the indignation generate the poetry.

EDNA ST. VINCENT MILLAY was born in Maine in 1892 and had written the famous "Renascence" before she attended Vassar College in 1913. Her intense feminism and hunger for beauty struck a responsive chord and she became the idol of more than one generation of rebellious young women. To modern poetry she brought a new freedom of mood and movement and an attractive bitter-sweetness. Critics who looked for major poetry to follow the flowering of Miss Millay's talent were disappointed by the somewhat archaic rhetoric of *Fatal Interview* and the studied literary slow-motion of *Conversation at Midnight.*

MARIANNE MOORE was editor of that focus of revolutionary writing, *The Dial,* from 1925 to 1929. She was born in Missouri in 1887 and now lives in Brooklyn. Her impressive *Selected Poems* was published in 1935 with a preface by T. S. Eliot who said: "Miss Moore is one of those few who have done the language some service in my lifetime . . . carrying on that struggle for the maintenance of a living speech, for the maintenance of its strength, its subtlety, for the preservation of quality of feeling, which must be kept up in every generation."

OGDEN NASH was born in 1902 and has worked in various advertising and editorial capacities, including a term on the staff of the *New Yorker,* where most of the horrific rhymes of *Hard Lines* and subsequent volumes first appeared. Lines like "The Bronx? No, thonx!" may not be immortal, but they will live until the things they hold up to ridicule become something new and less strange.

WILFRED OWEN was killed at the age of 25 in the battle for the Sambre Canal, November 4, 1918. He was, to quote the words of his friend, editor and fellow Englishman, Edmund Blunden, "one of those destined beings who, without pride of self, 'see, as from a tower, the end of all'. Outwardly he was quiet, unobtrusive, full of good sense; inwardly he could not help regarding the world with the dignity of a seer." A woman who knew him as a young officer, already tending toward a profound pacifism, describes his sensitive, acutely sympathetic nature: "Direct personal experience and individual development can hardly be said to have existed for him. He could only suffer, or rejoice, vicariously." Like Keats, he knew that he would be among the English poets after his death, but he never lived to see his single small volume in print. "He was a man of absolute integrity of mind," wrote Siegfried Sassoon, another poet-friend. "He never wrote his poems (as so many war poets did) to make the effect of a personal gesture." It is for this reason, perhaps, that few lack the perfection of greatness, and a choice among them must be arbitrary.

DOROTHY PARKER, who was born in New Jersey in 1893, is even more famous as a wit than as the author of the most acidulous *vers de societé* of her time. She claims to have learnt nothing at school "except that if you spit on a pencil eraser, it will erase ink." Superstitious, pessimistic, gregarious and something of a radical, she writes movie scenarios and short stories, as well as the verse recently collected in *Not So Deep as a Well.*

EZRA POUND, the *enfant terrible* of modern poetry, was born in Idaho in 1885 and has lived abroad (in London, Paris and Rapallo, Italy) since 1908. Instigator of movements—Imagism, Vorticism, Objectivism, Social Credit—the classic and oriental erudition, the conversational formalism of his art have exerted an acknowledged and profound influence on such widely different talents as Eliot, MacLeish, Hemingway, Ford Madox Ford, Joyce and Yeats. His early lyrics are fresh, but always faintly literary. His interminable *Cantos* are a badly assimilated potpourri of history, economics, science, and especially literature. At their best they rise to symphonic impressionism.

FREDERIC PROKOSCH was born in Wisconsin in 1909. He was educated at Harvard, Yale and Cambridge. Making something of a reputation at home and abroad as a scholar and champion squash-racquets player, his novels (*The Asiatics, The Seven Who Fled*) have been notable for an almost sickly response to the beauty of things past. The same feeling, intensified, inspires his poems.

JOHN CROWE RANSOM was born in Tennessee in 1888 and studied at Vanderbilt and Oxford Universities. He teaches at the former and has edited several publications (notably *The Fugitive*) devoted to the cultivation of letters in the South. With *Chills and Fever,* 1924, he set the pace for the elegant intellectualism that has stamped most Southern poetry since. The matter of his poems is trivial; the philosophy, ironic; the style, superbly deft.

LOLA RIDGE's radical, "class-conscious" poetry antedates by a generation most of the work commonly described in those terms. She was born in Ireland, coming to New York in 1907 and publishing *The Ghetto and Other Poems* in 1918. Her more recent long poems, tenuous and mystical, intense and unpopular, have tended to obscure the historical importance of her early inventions.

EDWIN ARLINGTON ROBINSON was born in Maine in 1869. He spent several years at Harvard and from 1893 to 1910 worked at a succession of clerical jobs in New York City, one of which he secured through President Theodore Roosevelt who had read *Captain Craig.* With *The Man Against the Sky,* Robinson's reputation as the master philosophic poet of his time was made. He began to present character, specifically the "little man" of the American lower middle class and farm, with a realism and economy new to American poetry. From then on, as Untermeyer remarks, "Frustration and defeat are like an organ-point heard below the varying music of his verse; failure is almost glorified." In later years, as Robinson turned out Tennysonian tragedies with a New England background to meet the cost of living-for-letters, his work became more bleakly moral, his blank verse more uncompromisingly spare. He died in 1935, a lonely man but praised and honored for his single-minded devotion to poetry.

SELDEN RODMAN was born in New York City in 1909 and graduated from Yale in 1931 where he founded and edited the polemical *Harkness Hoot* with William Harlan Hale. He is the author of *Mortal Triumph and Other Poems,* 1932, and *Lawrence: The Last Crusade,* 1937. With Alfred M. Bingham he edits the political monthly *Common Sense.*

EDWIN ROLFE, now serving with the International Brigade in Spain, was born in Philadelphia in 1909. Familiar with the labor movement from childhood, the proletarian quality of his verse is, in his case, no affectation. He has been at various times a clothing-cutter, machine tender, furniture worker and journalist, and his first book of poems, *To My Contemporaries,* was published by Dynamo Press in 1936.

MURIEL RUKEYSER's first book, *Theory of Flight,* was hailed in 1935 as "One of those rare first volumes which impress by their achievement more than by their promise." She was twenty-one at the time, born in New York, had attended Vassar and had already begun those travels to storm-centers of revolt from which the material for her best work has been invariably drawn. "Her poems," said Philip Blair

Rice, "not only present and celebrate experience, but evaluate it." And, added Stephen Vincent Benét, "When Miss Rukeyser speaks her politics—and she speaks with sincerity and fire—she does so like a poet, not like a slightly worn phonograph record." Not primarily a lyricist (her second book, *U.S.1*, is the preface to an ambitious evaluation of the Atlantic seaboard), her short poems have, none the less, much of the grave exaltation of Spender. Allowing for such defects as the too-lush condensation of *Theory of Flight* and the too-prosy documentation of *U.S.1* at the other extreme, Muriel Rukeyser's poetry has a physical quality present in few, if any, other women poets: not merely flesh and blood—but bones.

CARL SANDBURG was born in Illinois in 1878. He received his apprenticeship to the mantle of Walt Whitman in such varied occupations as reporter, scene-shifter, athlete, dish-washer, harvest hand, copy-writer, salesman, Socialist organizer, itinerant guitar-player and soldier in the Spanish-American War. Not until 1914, with the appearance of the famous "Chicago" in Harriet Monroe's *Poetry*, did he establish his reputation as a poet. Like Whitman, Sandburg employed the common speech of the people, including slang—but less self-consciously. Like Whitman also, his work was fired with a democratic zeal and an identification with the traditions of a growing country, especially the folklore of its receding frontier. His most recent collection, *The People, Yes*, has all of the salt and more sense of form than his earlier work. He is the author of the lyrical biography, *Abraham Lincoln: The Prairie Years*, and edited *The American Songbag*. He lives at Hobart, Michigan.

DELMORE SCHWARTZ was born in 1914 in Brooklyn and was educated at New York University and Harvard.

Precocious, versatile and productive, he had published verse, criticism, drama, short stories, written a novel, before his first collection of poems appeared in the autumn of 1938. In each of these media, Schwartz is predominantly concerned with "the values by which people live, as distinct from their beliefs and explicit avowals of choice." Particularly in his poems does one sense the tragic contrast between these values and the environment in which they must be brought to fruition.

STEPHEN SPENDER is one of the few poets whose first reviewers will not have cause to regret that they compared him to Shelley. Not that he has yet achieved the philosophic breadth of that poet's maturity—but the intensity with which he calls for comradeship and celebrates freedom strike a new high in the rich tradition of English lyricism. He was born in 1909, attended Oxford, has been closely associated with the Auden-Day Lewis group and with left-wing politics, has travelled widely on the Continent. The fluid-image technique of the oft-quoted

> Eye, gazelle, delicate wanderer,
> Drinker of horizon's fluid line . . .

has been criticized as symptomatic of the excess of ambiguity which is Spender's most obvious weakness. Sensitivity, verging on the feminine, a distrust of his own sentiment which too often leads to involved circumlocution—these tendencics cannot cfface the singing strength of a dozen unsurpassed outpourings.

WILLIAM STEPHENS, a former Gary and Chicago newspaperman now on the staff of *Esquire-Coronet*, was born in Utah in 1896. He has been active in the labor movement, particularly in the organization of the steel industry in 1936, and his poems have appeared in *Common Sense, Poetry, The Forum* and the *New Masses*. The first book Stephens is preparing for publication, to be entitled *Factory Models,* should establish his right to stand with those affirmative younger poets whose voices distinguish the new American poetry from the *malaise* of England's.

WALLACE STEVENS, who was born in Pennsylvania in 1879, and educated at Harvard, lives at Hartford, Connecticut. More than any other modern poet, he has constructed a complete dream world. But he insists, like Bishop Berkeley, that this world of ideas is the real one; and while the tools he uses have been fancy, barbaric color, irony, abstraction and archaism, it must be admitted that the mortar itself has been the incongruous data of contemporary urban life. *Harmonium, Ideas of Order* and *The Man with the Blue Guitar* comprise his contribution to a difficult genre.

ALLEN TATE was born in Kentucky in 1899 and lives in Tennessee. His *Selected Poems* were recently published and he is the author of *Reactionary Essays* as well as biographies of Jefferson Davis and Stonewall Jackson. A Southern Agrarian in his politics, Tate's writing primly combines the "wit" of Pope and Donne with the uneasy modern conscience of T. S. Eliot.

WALTER JAMES TURNER was born in Australia in 1889 and lives in England, where he has been literary, musical and dramatic critic on such journals as the *London Mercury* and the *Daily Herald*. He has written novels, plays, satire and criticism. His poems, partly delightful fantasy, part an attempt to fix the poetry of science, are comparable, especially in their compact phrasing, to those of Wallace Stevens.

BARTOLOMEO VANZETTI was born in Italy in 1888. He landed at Ellis Island at the age of 20 and during the years until his arrest in 1919, he worked in stone-pits, brick-yards, construction gangs and ice-works; finally as a carpenter and fish-peddler. A passionate student and thinker during this period (*The Divine Comedy* and Renan's *Jesus* were his favorite books) he turned from the catholicism of his up-bringing to theories of radical social change. It was as a philosophic anarchist and an active labor leader that he was framed on a murder charge with Nicola Sacco during the post-war red-hysteria. He spent seven years in jail and was electrocuted August 22, 1927.

JAMES PALMER WADE was born in 1909 and lives near Knoxville, Tennessee. Though handicapped by a serious defect of hearing, he made a name for himself with his stories and poems the very year he entered Yale in 1927. He has written two novels since graduation, been a member of the Federal Writers Project of the WPA, and contributed his unique symbolist verse to such magazines as *Poetry*.

OSCAR WILLIAMS began writing poetry for the second time in 1937. His first and only book, *The Golden Darkness*, was published in 1921 when he was 22 years of age by the Yale University Press. During the intervening years, he says, he "neither wrote nor read," but worked as an advertising and promotion expert for a number of firms, his last assignment being Chairman for Advertising of the State Democratic Party of Florida in 1936. His ingenuity in devising red, white and blue ads. for the local papers was a factor in the election of Governor Fred P. Cone. Having dropped his writing in 1921 from a sense of futility at the gulf between poet and public, he resumed in the belief that he was prepared eventually "to write a poem that would *act*—that would walk off the table and perform."

WILLIAM CARLOS WILLIAMS was born in 1883 and lives at Rutherford, New Jersey, where he practises medicine. The prose of his recently published novel, *White Mule,* and the short stories, *Life Along the Passaic,* has been called "surgical"—both for its precision and its insistence upon physical detail. But in Williams' poems, which have agitated literary circles for two decades, there is an additional quality—the bird-like lyricism of the usually clipped lines, in which "anti-poetic" language is deliberately used to achieve contrast and new poetic meaning.

E. B. WHITE was born in Mt. Vernon, New York, in 1899 and has been editor of the *New Yorker* since that lively magazine's inception. If wittier, more apparently effortless comedy has been achieved in our time than the ballad satirizing Rivera's attempt to paint Lenin on the walls of Mr. Rockefeller's City—this anthologist would like to see it. Yet, when pressed for an explanation, Mr. White said: "Writing light verse is very heavy work indeed; I get just as exhausted as the major poets."

ELINOR WYLIE was born in New Jersey in 1885 and died in New York in 1928. Her family, like her poetry, was aristocratic. She lived in England for some years, after shocking Washington society with a succession of impulsive marriages. Her novels, as well as her poems, won an early distinction for their meticulous grace and exquisite subjective perceptions. As the influence of "metaphysical" poets like Donne became more pronounced, and her emotional life deepened, Elinor Wylie came very close to giving her intensely personal idiom a universal elevation. But in spite of her fine craftsmanship, this poet is destined to remain an essentially feminine talent.

W. B. YEATS may be properly compared to Goethe for the increasing development of his art during a long lifetime, and for the energy with which, almost single-handed, he stimulated the birth of a whole national literature. Born in Ireland in 1865, living at times in Paris and London, Yeats was associated with Oscar Wilde, Mallarmé and George Moore as a young man; later, as dramatist, with Synge, O'Casey and Lady Gregory; then with Joyce and AE and Pound; finally with Eliot and Auden and Turner. His early poems were dreamily impressionistic. He was a mystic, and even devoted himself to spiritualism for a while. Then he stripped his verse of vague ornament, originating a conversational, but always precise style, to convey more intellectual concepts. But throughout, Yeats has been and remains the high priest of symbolism. Recently he has dealt with politics in his poems, but in an ironic, detached manner. Whether the winner of the 1924 Nobel Prize will make still another sphere of poetic interest his own in the eighth decade of an astonishing life may be doubted, but generations of poets unborn will look back with pride upon the fathomless reserve of spirit still affirming at 70

> That I may seem, though I die old,
> A foolish, passionate man . . .

Index of First Lines

Alphabetical List of Poets